FEVER-TREE

THE ART OF MIXING

SIMPLE LONG DRINKS & COCKTAILS
FROM THE WORLD'S LEADING BARS

MITCHELL BEAZLEY

An Hachette UK Company
www.hachette.co.uk

First published in Great Britain in 2017 by Mitchell Beazley, a division of
Octopus Publishing Group Ltd
Carmelite House
50 Victoria Embankment
London EC4Y 0DZ
www.octopusbooks.co.uk

Distributed in the US by Hachette Book Group
1290 Avenue of the Americas
4th and 5th Floors, New York, NY 10020

Distributed in Canada by Canadian Manda Group
664 Annette Street, Toronto, Ontario, Canada M6S 2C8

ISBN 978-1-78472-189-3

A CIP catalogue record for this book is available from the British Library.

Printed and bound in Italy

10 9 8 7 6

All recipes serve one unless otherwise stated.
Eggs should be medium unless otherwise stated. The Department
of Health advises that eggs should not be consumed raw. This book
contains drinks made with raw eggs. It is prudent for more vulnerable
people such as pregnant and nursing mothers, invalids, the elderly,
babies and young children to avoid uncooked or lightly cooked recipes
made with eggs. Once prepared these drinks should be consumed promptly.

Additional picture credits
Alamy Stock Photo Javier Etcheverry 182. Getty Images Zubin Shroff 71.
Fever-Tree 5, 6, 8, 15, 16, 19, 67, 69, 129, 131, 179, 180.

Group Publishing Director Denise Bates
Consultant Editor Sarah Ford
Senior Editor Pauline Bache
Art Director Yasia Williams-Leedham
Designer Geoff Fennell
Marketing Director (for Fever-Tree) Saskia Meyer
International Marketing Coordinator (for Fever-Tree) Andrew Harris
Photographer Paul Winch-Furness
Mixologist Missy Flynn
Stylist Jennifer Kay
Senior Production Manager Katherine Hockley

CONTENTS

INTRODUCTION

BY CHARLES ROLLS & TIM WARRILLOW

This book contains more than 125 simple recipes for delicious long drinks, created for us by bartenders around the world, to make for yourself and your friends at home.

Long drinks combining spirits and mixers have obviously been around for many, many years. And with good reason. They quench the thirst, revive the spirit and are refreshingly simple to make – usually involving just three ingredients – spirit, mixer and garnish.

Their very simplicity has led to their huge resurgence in popularity with both bartenders and at home. They are simple, but also delicious, because of the availability of an exciting range of quality spirits that have appeared on the market over the last few years. Fortunately Fever-Tree came along as well, because before that there were no premium mixers to match the quality of the best spirits. And when we say premium, at Fever-Tree that is all down to one word:

Quality.

Fever-Tree began with one simple idea: if three-quarters of your Gin and Tonic is going to be tonic, wouldn't you want it to be the very best tonic that tonic could be? In this introduction, we're going to tell you why that is so important. (Although, if you're thirsty right now, please jump ahead and mix up a storm – or perhaps a Continental Storm (*see* page 110), Mattias Skoog's twist on a Dark & Stormy – you can always check in with our story later on...)

We (Charles and Tim) would never have pursued the Fever-Tree idea were it not for the boom in the market for "premium spirits" that has grown steadily over the last 30 years.

"Premium" is obviously a relative term, but it suggests quality. In some categories, such as gin, this quality is relatively easy to discern. Non-premium products will let themselves down very obviously, either by being flavoured with essences rather than distilled with botanicals, or by having a poor base spirit or too little alcohol – gin

The fertile slopes of Mount Etna in Sicily are peppered with idyllic lemon groves.

Tim sets to work harvesting quinine by beating the bark off a cinchona branch.

requires a minimum of 40 per cent ABV to anchor any botanicals other than juniper into its structure. Here, newer products will be quickly found out if they don't match up.

For many years, single malt whiskies had defined premium spirits along with high-end cognac and Armagnac. Then, for a while in the 1990s, vodka was the hot category, with super-premium brands like Belvedere and Chopin making names for themselves by arguing the merits of distilling with rye or potatoes respectively. More recently it has been gin's turn along with tequila, while rum, the perennial party spirit, has enjoyed a slow renaissance since the launch of El Dorado premium quality aged rums in 1992.

However, what we focused on when we first met, was that no one had taken this approach with mixers. Spirits were where the love and attention, the craft, had been focused, while mixers remained broadly ignored. In fact, more than ignored – debased.

By the late 1970s, the world's leading producers of tonic water were losing market share to cheaper, lower-end products. To preserve their business, they fought back by cutting costs, joining their rivals in using cheaper ingredients so that they could lower their price to compete. In Britain, this meant, for example, replacing cane sugar with saccharine. In the United States, they began using high-fructose corn syrup. In addition, cheaper essential oils replaced the originals. All of this was to the detriment of quality and flavour, which matters. Because, to paraphrase James Carville, Bill Clinton's erstwhile political guru, what makes a great drink? *It's the ingredients, stupid...*

We decided that, for Fever-Tree, there would be no compromise. Flavour and quality would be everything. And that meant that we would have to find the very best ingredients for our products. In the case of tonic water, our signature mixer, that meant no saccharine but natural cane sugar; no decanal but proper bitter orange essential oils. And proper, natural quinine. It's a decision that has led us from the bookish environment of the British Library in Euston to our facing the wrong end of a Kalashnikov in the

Charles samples the aromas of the finest lemon thyme in Provence.

deepest jungles of Africa. And it's been worth every second.

While we began with tonic water – we take our name from one of the many given to the cinchona tree, from which the natural quinine is extracted – we always set out to bring quality back to the overall mixer category. Year on year, we have sought to bring out something new, from our flavoured range of tonics to ginger ale, ginger beer, lemonade and cola, including a range of mixers aimed explicitly at the dark spirits market, for whisky, rum and brandy. For the premium blends, these mixers will extend the occasions when great spirits can be enjoyed.

Each new product has brought its own challenges, both in terms of sourcing the ingredients and then guaranteeing their supply. (Later in the book, we'll relate some of our adventures hunting quinine in Democratic Republic of the Congo, ginger in Ivory Coast and vanilla in Madagascar, and tell you about the committed farmers who grow and refine them.) But we have always believed that, if we made mixers with the very best products available, the market would respond.

We wanted nothing less than revolution – to disrupt one of the most forgotten and uncared for sectors of the drinks industry.

This idea is at the heart of our philosophy: we want to make the best mixers it is possible to make.

Our greatest allies in the Fever-Tree project have been the bartenders, chefs, sommeliers, spirits makers and drinks writers who have embraced our mixers and who have become ambassadors. We are very grateful to them all and this book is our chance to thank them for supporting our adventure. It has taken us from the rolling herb fields of Provence to the slopes of Mount Etna, from the Gloucestershire countryside to the heart of Africa.

And all because, ten years ago, we wanted a decent Gin and Tonic...it's staggering the lengths a couple of chaps will go to for that.

Charles Rolls and Tim Warrillow

EQUIPMENT
TOOLS & GLASSES

These tools are worth investing in to make the cocktails in this book.

Cocktail shaker: the Boston shaker is the simplest option, but it needs to be used in conjunction with a hawthorne strainer. Alternatively, you could choose a shaker with a built-in strainer.

Muddler: similar to a pestle, which will work just as well, this is used to crush fruit or herbs in a glass or shaker for drinks like a Mojito.

Bar spoon: similar to a teaspoon but with a long handle, a bar spoon is used for stirring, layering and muddling drinks.

Measuring tool or jigger: this will ensure the correct proportions in your cocktails.

Hawthorne or tea strainer: to strain bits of ingredients and shards of ice out of your drink. A hawthorne strainer (consisting of a handled metal disc with a spring wound around the edge) works well with a Boston shaker but you can use a tea strainer, too.

GLASSES

The glass that you use depends on the type of drink you are making, with long drinks requiring a tall glass (like a highball or collins) and shorter drinks requiring a shorter glass (such as a rocks glass). Stemmed glasses can be used for cocktails served without ice or Spanish-inspired styles (as the traditional Spanish method of serving a G&T is in a wine glass). Here are the basic glass styles used in this book.

Highball: a tall glass with straight sides, perfect for most long drinks.

Goblet: a stemmed glass with a large bowl.

Rocks: also known as an old fashioned glass, this is a short glass with a wide brim.

Collins: a narrower and slightly taller glass than a highball.

Burgundy or red wine: a large, stemmed wine glass, also referred to as a large balloon wine glass.

White wine: a slightly shorter glass, with a smaller bowl than a Burgundy or red wine glass.

Margarita: a stemmed glass with a wide bowl and a stepped diameter.

Sling: a tall glass with a narrow base and wider rim.

Mixing: a wide-bottomed, large glass with sturdy sides used for mixing and cooling drinks quickly. Not to be used to serve drinks in.

Coupette: a saucer-shaped, stemmed glass.

Champagne flute: a tall, stemmed glass with a narrow rim to prolong the fizz of a drink.

Julep cup: short metal cup, usually with a handle.

TECHNIQUES
MIXING, INGREDIENTS & GARNISHES

Mastering these simple techniques will enable you to make a plethora of cocktails and mixed drinks.

Shaking: used to mix ingredients thoroughly and to chill the drink before serving. Shaken cocktails are usually shaken with ice cubes to cool the drink without diluting it and then strained to remove any shards of ice. Shake until a frost forms on the outside of the shaker.

Stirring: a cocktail is stirred when the ingredients need to be mixed and chilled but it's also important to maintain the clarity with no air bubbles or fragmented ice.

Muddling: used to bring out the flavours of herbs and fruit using a muddler. To muddle, add the ingredients to be muddled to a mixing glass. Hold the glass firmly and use the muddler to press down on the ingredients. Twist and press to release the flavours. Continue for about 30 seconds, then follow the recipe accordingly.

Frosting: a sugar- or salt-frosted rim adds a professional look to a cocktail. To add a frosting, dip the rim of the glass in a saucer of lime or lemon juice or water. Spread the sugar or salt on a small plate and place the rim of the glass in the frosting. Twist to give an even coating and use a lime or lemon wedge to clean off any excess frosting from inside of the glass to prevent it from contaminating the cocktail. If you want to be sure that the frosting will stay in place, use egg white in place of the citrus juice to stick the sugar or salt to the glass.

Double straining: used when you want to prevent all traces of puréed fruit and ice fragments from entering the glass. To double-strain, simply use two straining methods, such as a shaker with a built-in strainer in conjunction with a hawthorne strainer. Alternatively, strain through a fine strainer.

Making a twist: a citrus twist garnish looks good and imparts flavour to the cocktail. Pare a strip of peel from the fruit and remove all signs of pith. Twist the peel over the surface of the drink to release the oils (known as expressing the peel), then drop it into the drink. Flaming the peel before twisting it releases even more flavour.

Dehydrating garnishes: dehydrated fruits, vegetables and fruit peels can be used to garnish a drink. Make them in a specialist dehydrator or in a very low-heated oven (50°C/120°F). Slice the fruit or vegetable very thinly to dehydrate it properly and if the recipe calls for dehydrated fruit peel, use unwaxed peel and remove as much of the white pith as possible.

Check the oven or dehydrator every 30 minutes, until the fruit is firm.

Making simple sugar syrup: You can buy sugar syrup or make your own by mixing equal parts caster sugar and boiling water, then stirring until dissolved. Homemade sugar syrup will keep in a sterilized bottle in the refrigerator for up to 2 weeks. This method and equal parts ratio also works to create demerera, agave, honey and muscovado syrups.

QUININE
FEVER-TREE TONIC WATER

Let us be in no doubt: tonic water is the drink that changed the world. And it is all thanks to quinine.

Quinine is a medical miracle. Its effects were to the 19th century what penicillin's were to the 20th. However, where penicillin is relatively easy to make, quinine was much harder to acquire.

ORIGINS

Quinine comes from the bark of the cinchona tree, which is native to the foothills of the High Andes. Here, its properties were known for generations and when Europeans arrived and also fell ill with the fevers, the local population shared their knowledge. It wasn't long before quinine became one of the most valuable exports from the Americas. It was hardly surprising, then, that the emerging nations of Peru and its neighbours were desperate to maintain their monopoly on cinchona, and outlawed the export of its seeds and seedlings.

In this, they had one useful advantage: the cinchona tree is not only rare, it is also very hard to grow. The trees are particular. They prefer a cool climate, but they cannot stand frost. They don't like the temperature to fluctuate too much between summer and winter or night and day. They don't like stagnant moisture around their roots, so good drainage is important. And they don't like direct sunlight.

THE MAGIC BULLET

But that wasn't going to stop other people trying to acquire the trees and to grow them themselves. To European colonists, eyeing India, Africa and South East Asia for future exploitation, this was the magic bullet they had been waiting for for their military advantage. Hitherto, the British and French armies had been decimated by malaria. But with quinine, their ambitions could be realized.

So, like Victorian Indiana Joneses, plant hunters and botanists set forth to raid the jungles of Amazonia and beyond in an attempt to steal plants and seedlings. And in 1865, the Briton Charles Ledger succeeded, smuggling seeds out of the Bolivian rain forest.

Now the race was on to see who would be the first to farm cinchona commercially. Half of Ledger's seeds went to India, where they failed to take hold. The other half went to Java, then controlled by the Dutch, where they thrived.

Tonic water is the drink that changed the world.

Harvesting quinine is a careful, old-fashioned and drawn out process.

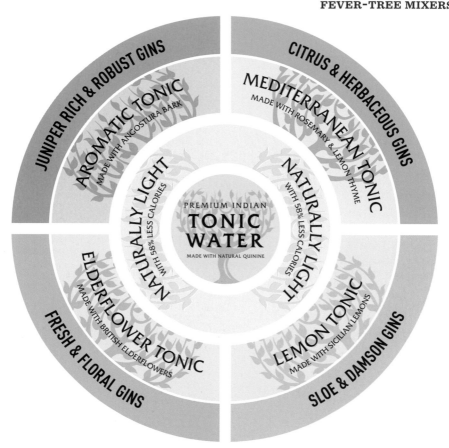

JUNIPER RICH & ROBUST GINS

CITRUS & HERBACEOUS GINS

AROMATIC TONIC
MADE WITH ANGOSTURA BARK

MEDITERRANEAN TONIC
MADE WITH ROSEMARY & LEMON THYME

NATURALLY LIGHT
WITH 58% LESS CALORIES

NATURALLY LIGHT
WITH 58% LESS CALORIES

PREMIUM INDIAN
TONIC
WATER
MADE WITH NATURAL QUININE

ELDERFLOWER TONIC
MADE WITH BRITISH ELDERFLOWERS

LEMON TONIC
MADE WITH SICILIAN LEMONS

FRESH & FLORAL GINS

SLOE & DAMSON GINS

BEYOND G&T

While Gin and Tonic can rightly claim to be one of the world's most popular mixed long drinks, that doesn't mean that other spirits don't play well with tonic water. And we don't just mean vodka. Tonic water pairs well with rum, tequila and countless others. So, in addition to the classic G&T and those versions with ingenious twists that follow, there are plenty more experiments to do, including a T&T (*see* page 24) and a delicious combination with Aperol and fino sherry (*see* page 30).

With a ready supply of a malarial prophylactic assured, to be taken daily, ideally in tonic water, Europe's so-called Scramble for Africa began in earnest. By the 1840s, the British in India were refining and consuming more than 700 tonnes of cinchona bark annually to prevent malaria.

A CHALLENGING TASTE

There was, however, one substantial problem. Quinine has to be taken orally and it tastes unpalatably bitter. When we received our very first sample of the quinine we now use, Tim made the mistake of dipping his finger in it and dabbing it on his tongue! The best solution was to mix it in water and citrus and balance out its bitterness with sugar. And thus tonic water was born. (Adding gin helped, too.)

When we began making tonic, one of our first goals was to restore quinine to its proper place in our recipe. All we had to do was find the best quinine we could, ideally from the original *ledgeriana* trees descended from those Charles Ledger had taken from Peru so many years ago.

After much research, we found some.

In 1933, Prince Leopold of Belgium sent a small tin of *ledgeriana* seeds to the Belgian Congo. Its high hills and mild climate, so similar to that of the Andes, make it perfect cinchona country. But the surviving plantations, on the border between Rwanda

THE TASTEMAKERS

In 2007 Charles and Tim found themselves sitting in the world renowned Spanish restaurant, elBulli, eating a dish prepared by head chef Ferran Adriá called "sopa de tonica Fever-Tree". ElBulli had been voted the world's best restaurant for the second year in a row.

Adriá had recently discovered Fever-Tree and, approaching Charles and Tim at the table, exclaimed "you have created a tonic that has helped to perfect the Spanish chef's favourite drink – the gin tonic!" He was the first of many expert taste makers around the world to recommend Fever-Tree, and his and many others' endorsement have been central to raising awareness of Fever-Tree around the world.

and the Democratic Republic of the Congo, lie in one of the most anarchic corners of the world: Bukavu. At the time of Tim's visit the UK Foreign and Commonwealth Office's advice to travellers on the area boiled down to "don't go". And yet, somehow, one family continue to extract the purest natural source of quinine.

As impressed as we were by their sample – the same one that Tim had tasted – we both knew we had to be sure that they would be able to meet our requirements in the long term. Which meant that one of us had to travel to Bukavu. Since Charles had already crossed Central Africa before (and caught malaria), Tim drew the short straw.

What he found there is little short of remarkable. Bukavu lies on the Ruzizi River Kivu, which marks the Democratic Republic of the Congo's border with Rwanda. It is one of the most fertile places on earth. It is also one of the most dangerous, where political control oscillates frequently. There is little more than the factory, a brewery, the DHL office

and the world's best cinchona producers. Their 28 cinchona plantations spread like vineyards all over the mountains, with trees harvested when they are about eight or nine years old, and new seedlings planted in their place. Harvesting the quinine is an old-fashioned and drawn-out process. Once the trees are felled, the bark is beaten off into dry cloth where it dries for two to three weeks. Then, once the humidity and quinine content have been measured, the bark is put into a hammer mill, ground and soaked in acid. The resulting liquid is filtered and evaporated until only the quinine remains.

Ours is the only tonic water to contain this purest natural source of quinine. It is the lynchpin ingredient. Perhaps it didn't take quite so long to find our quinine as it took Charles Ledger to find his seeds. But, for a while there, it felt like it.

When we began making tonic, one of our first goals was to restore quinine to its proper place in our recipe.

The stunning view from the cinchona plantation in Bukavu.

THE CLASSICS

ULTIMATE GIN & TONIC

**Make sure you are quick when adding
your garnish as you want that fizz to
tickle your nose as you smell the aromas
of Gin and Tonic. Drink and enjoy.**
(Pictured overleaf centre)

50ml (2fl oz) premium gin
200ml (7fl oz) Fever-Tree Indian
　　Tonic Water
Twist of lime peel, to garnish

*Add the gin to a tall glass over ice cubes,
followed by the tonic water. Twist the lime
peel over the glass, to release the oils, before
dropping it into the drink.*

CAMPARI & TONIC

**Substituting Campari for gin gives
an Italian and colourful option. The
bitter nature of Campari, which is not
juniper based, is well loved by many. It
is made from a secret infusion of herbs,
plants, fruits, water and alcohol, and has
become synonymous with Italian bar
culture. With estimates of the number
of ingredients ranging from 20 to 80,
this mysterious mix is a bitter-sweet
taste sensation.**
(Pictured overleaf left)

50ml (2fl oz) Campari
150ml (5fl oz) Fever-Tree Indian
　　Tonic Water
Lemon or orange wedge, to garnish

*Add the Campari to a highball glass over ice
cubes, followed by the tonic water. Garnish
with a lemon or orange wedge.*

GIN TONIC DE BARCELONA

The ingredients for this lovely summer drink are lightly muddled together to release all the flavours into the glass. It's packed full of fresh fruit aromas, with grapefruit, lemon and mint working together to create a balance of sour and sweet. Tonic water tops up the glass to lengthen the drink and dilute the gin to just the right sipping consistency.

(Pictured overleaf right)

60ml (4 tbsp) premium gin
1 large piece of grapefruit peel
1 large piece of lemon peel
Fever-Tree Indian Tonic Water, to top up
1 mint sprig, to garnish

Put all the ingredients except the mint and tonic water into a goblet and lightly muddle. Add ice cubes, top up with the tonic water and stir 4 times. Garnish with a mint sprig.

Bar: AUTRE MONDE – CHICAGO, USA

Bar person: BECCI WEST

GIN & TONIC (ESPAÑA STYLE)

We serve our Gin and Tonic in a large balloon wine glass, the way it is served all over Spain. As soon as a person orders one, we know we are going to be making five more, as it's so pretty that others decide to try it. We use Martin Miller's Gin, which is juniper rich and combines beautifully with the Indian tonic water, along with the muddled lime, mint and cucumber.

3–4 mint leaves
2 slices of cucumber
2 slices of lime
Splash of simple sugar syrup (see page 13)
45ml (3 tbsp) Martin Miller's Gin
Fever-Tree Indian Tonic Water, to top up

Muddle the mint, cucumber, lime and syrup in a mixing glass. Place a large, square ice cube in a large balloon wine glass. Add the gin, muddled fruit, and more (smaller) ice cubes, then top up with the tonic water.

Left: **CAMPARI & TONIC** – *see page 20*
Centre: **ULTIMATE GIN & TONIC** – *see page 20*
Right: **GIN TONIC DE BARCELONA** – *see page 21*

THE DUKE OF CARNUNTUM

First settled by the Ancient Romans, Carnuntum in Austria is rich in cultural history, and Pontica Vermouth is made of the wines that are produced there. This is a very grown-up cocktail with distinct flavours in the finished drink. Light tonic balances out the bitters and the orange zest brings out the sweetness of the vermouth. The relatively low alcohol content makes this the ideal daytime cocktail for those who wish to steer clear of more alcoholic drinks. *(Pictured overleaf right)*

50ml (2fl oz) Pontica Red Vermouth
1 dash of Peychaud's Bitters, or 1 tsp
   absinthe
Fever-Tree Indian Tonic Water, to top up
Twist of orange peel, to garnish

Pour the vermouth, Peychaud's Bitters or absinthe into a chilled Burgundy glass over ice cubes and top up with the tonic water. Garnish with a twist of orange peel.

ULTIMATE TEQUILA & TONIC

This is about as simple as a cocktail can be and yet you'll be surprised by the depth and complexity of the flavours that can be achieved with just two ingredients. The tonic water is packed full of botanicals that draw out the best from the tequila. The garnish is as simple and effective as the drink – a lime wedge that adds a splash of colour and citrus flavour. *(Pictured overleaf centre)*

50ml (2fl oz) premium white tequila
125ml (4fl oz) Fever-Tree Indian
   Tonic Water
Lime wedge, to garnish

Pour the tequila and tonic water into a highball glass over ice cubes. Garnish with a lime wedge.

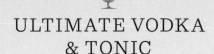

RÉMY GRAND TONIC

A French twist on the Gin and Tonic, this is an elegant, fresh summer drink.
(Pictured overleaf left)

50ml (2fl oz) Rémy Martin VSOP Mature
    Cask Finish Cognac
10ml (2 tsp) dry vermouth
125ml (4fl oz) Fever-Tree Indian
    Tonic Water
Lemon wedge, to garnish

Pour the cognac and vermouth into a Burgundy glass over ice cubes. Top up with the tonic water and garnish with a lemon wedge.

ULTIMATE VODKA & TONIC

This is a classic long drink that lets the natural flavours of our tonic water really shine through.

50ml (2fl oz) premium vodka
200ml (7fl oz) Fever-Tree Indian
    Tonic Water
Twist of lemon peel, to garnish

Pour the vodka into a tall glass over ice cubes, followed by the tonic water. Twist the lemon peel over the drink, to release the oils, before dropping it into the drink.

METAXA & TONIC

This smooth, amber-coloured Greek spirit blends perfectly with tonic to create a delicious, summery, long drink.

50ml (2fl oz) Metaxa 5 Stars
200ml (7fl oz) Fever-Tree Indian
    Tonic Water
Orange slice, to garnish

Pour the Metaxa 5 Stars into a highball glass over ice cubes. Top up with the tonic water and garnish with an orange slice.

LILLET & TONIC

Lillet provided a quinine fix for France's colonial troops in Africa as tonic did for British troops in India in the 1800s.

50ml (2fl oz) Lillet Blanc, Rosé or Rouge
100ml (3½fl oz) Fever-Tree Indian
    Tonic Water
Lime or orange slice, to garnish

Fill a wine glass with plenty of ice cubes. Add the Lillet and tonic water and garnish with a lime or orange slice.

Left: **RÉMY GRAND TONIC**
— *see page 25*
Centre: **ULTIMATE TEQUILA**
& TONIC — *see page 24*
Right: **THE DUKE OF CARNUNTUM**
— *see page 24*

GARDEN VARIETY G&T

As Hendrick's Gin is infused with cucumber and rose petal, I added celery bitters and rosewater to emphasize its characteristics. The name reflects the scent of the cocktail and reminds the drinker of an English country garden. It has a really light and refreshing taste that's highlighted with the cucumber garnish – fresh, clean and pure.
(Pictured)

45ml (3 tbsp) Hendrick's Gin
1 dash of celery bitters (optional)
3 drops of rosewater
90ml (3fl oz) Fever-Tree Indian Tonic Water
Cucumber slice, to garnish

Pour all the ingredients except the tonic water into a tumbler or collins glass over ice cubes. Top up with the tonic water and gently stir. Garnish with a cucumber slice.

BRIDGETOWN TWIST

Named after the capital city of Barbados, where this incredible rum hails from, this is a sunshine drink with a Caribbean kick. Lime juice and rum are natural partners, and the addition of vermouth brings yet another layer to the drink. We add a little simple sugar syrup – taste as you go and try to create the ideal balance between the sour and sweet flavours. Then top up with tonic for the perfect evening drink.

35ml (2 generous tbsp) Mount Gay Rum, or other premium golden rum
15ml (1 tbsp) lime juice
12.5ml (2½ tsp) sweet dry vermouth
100ml (3½fl oz) Fever-Tree Indian Tonic Water
Simple sugar syrup, to taste (*see* page 13)

Pour all the ingredients in order into a highball glass over ice cubes. Stir to mix and serve simply without a garnish.

APE & PEPE

The unusual name of this drink comes from its key ingredients – Ape for Aperol and Pepe for Tio Pepe. We wanted to create a cocktail for our terrace menu that would look as delicate as it tastes. Sherry and Aperol are the stars of this drink and then we add some lemon juice for a sour note, to work with the other flavours. Syrup adds the sweetness and a dash of peach bitters is an optional addition that will add a really unique undertone to the drink. The overall taste is tart and dry yet really refreshing.

25ml (5 tsp) Aperol
25ml (5 tsp) Tio Pepe fino sherry
25ml (5 tsp) fresh lemon juice
25ml (5 tsp) homemade chamomile syrup (see below)
1 dash of The Bitter Truth Peach Bitters (optional)
Fever-Tree Indian Tonic Water, to top up
Orange wheel, to garnish
Mint sprig, to garnish

Chamomile syrup (makes 1 litre/34fl oz)
1kg (2lb 4oz) granulated sugar
10g (¼oz) dried chamomile (from a chamomile tea bag)

To make the chamomile syrup, dissolve the sugar in 1 litre (34fl oz) of boiling water in a saucepan. Add the chamomile and boil for a few minutes. Cool at room temperature for 4 hours, then strain the syrup into a sterilized bottle. Store in the refrigerator for up to 1 month.

To make the cocktail, pour all the ingredients except the tonic water into a cocktail shaker and give it a good, hard shake, then double-strain over ice into a white wine glass and top up with the tonic water. Garnish with an orange wheel and a mint sprig.

FANCIFUL G&T

As this drink is a fanciful G&T, it is worth keeping the name simple to communicate to people exactly what they are getting: something slightly more interesting than a standard G&T, yet not quite a cocktail. The drink highlights the complex nature of Four Pillars Rare Dry Gin and the tonic water balances ideally with the spice and citrus flavours of the gin, allowing its best characters to come through, as it isn't too overpowering. This is a particularly refreshing tipple that's perfect as a light afternoon drink or a cleansing nightcap. *(Pictured overleaf left)*

4 frozen blueberries
50ml (2fl oz) Four Pillars Rare Dry Gin
150ml (5fl oz) Fever-Tree Indian
    Tonic Water
Apple slices, to garnish
Bay leaf (optional), to garnish

Put the blueberries and gin into a Burgundy wine glass or goblet. Top up with ice cubes and add the tonic water.

To make the apple fan garnish, skewer 6 slices of apple on to a cocktail stick and spread the slices out into a fan shape. Add to the drink, with a bay leaf if liked, and serve immediately.

MILANO

This is a cocktail that's inspired by life in Milan, hence the Aperol and coffee. We also like to add cold-brewed coffee in cocktails and therefore we wanted to create a special drink for the bar that included the slightly acidic notes of coffee. This is a long drink served in a highball glass but, as it's not too heavy on alcohol, it can be enjoyed at any time as a pick-me-up or apéritif. *(Pictured overleaf right)*

50ml (2fl oz) coffee-infused Aperol (*see* below)
100–120ml (3½–4fl oz) Fever-Tree Indian Tonic Water
Lemon wheel, to garnish

Coffee-infused Aperol
100ml (3½fl oz) Arabica coffee beans
700ml (1½ pints) bottle of Aperol

To make the coffee-infused Aperol, pour the coffee beans into the Aperol bottle and leave to infuse for 45 minutes. Strain and discard the coffee beans.

To make the cocktail, add the coffee-infused Aperol and then the tonic water to a highball or sling glass over large ice cubes. Garnish with a lemon wheel and serve with a spoon.

Left: **FANCIFUL G&T**
— *see page 32*
Right: **MILANO** — *see page 33*

COMMONWEALTH CUP

This cocktail is called the Commonwealth Cup because of the ingredients. It includes lots of different flavour sensations that come together to produce a refreshing drink with a citrusy garnish. The gin is infused with Earl Grey tea, which adds an aromatic element to this sophisticated drink. Lime juice is added and this sourness is complemented by a good dash of homemade honey syrup.

30ml (2 tbsp) Earl Grey-infused Martin Miller's Gin (*see below*)
30ml (2 tbsp) white wine (a sauvignon blanc works well)
10ml (2 tsp) homemade honey syrup (*see* page 13)
2 lime wedges
10ml (2 tsp) Fever-Tree Indian Tonic Water
Lime slice, to garnish

Earl Grey-infused gin (makes 700ml/ 1½ pints)
3 tsp Earl Grey tea leaves
700ml (1½ pints) Martin Miller's Gin

To make the Earl Grey-infused gin, add the tea leaves to the gin and leave to infuse for at least 1 hour. Strain to remove the tea leaves. The infusion will keep in a sterlized and sealed bottle in a cool, dark place for 4 weeks.

To make the cocktail, pour the gin, white wine and honey syrup into a highball glass over ice. Squeeze over the lime wedges, then drop them into the glass. Add the tonic water and garnish with a lime slice.

INDIAN AUTUMN

We wanted to do something classic, not a Gin and Tonic, with our own twist. So we came up with a vermouth and tonic. We use fresh juice from in-season mandarins and the tonic is room temperature, not chilled. As The Jane is a Michelin-starred restaurant, this is a fairly complex recipe but the nice bitterness of the Fever-Tree Indian Tonic combines well with the fruitiness of the mandarin. You can use any dry or red vermouth. These quantities make two drinks.

500ml (18fl oz) fresh, strained mandarin juice

Seeds from 1 vanilla pod

Zest of 1 mandarin

Juice of ½ a lime

120ml (4fl oz) Yzaguirre Dry Reserva Vermouth, or any dry vermouth

40ml (1¼fl oz) Vermut Falset Red Vermouth

2 leaves of gelatine

Fever-Tree Indian Tonic Water, at room temperature, to top up

Mix all the ingredients except the gelatine and tonic water in a large bowl that will fit in your freezer. Soak the gelatine in cold water in a small bowl for a few minutes until softened, then squeeze out the excess water. Gently heat a little of the mandarin mixture in a small saucepan and stir in the softened gelatine until dissolved. Pour the gelatine mixture into the mandarin mixture and stir to evenly disperse the vanilla. Put the bowl in the freezer and leave for about 4 hours until frozen. Remove the granita from the freezer, mix thoroughly with a fork, then spoon into a rocks glass. Top up with the tonic water.

MISSIONARY'S FORTUNE

Pairing dry rum flavours with sweet peach is one of my go-to combos when someone asks for something off the cuff. This is kind of a strange twist on a Missionary's Downfall with lots going on in relatively few ingredients. The choice of rum is important, as is the quality of the tonic water, as these will determine the ultimate flavours that are derived from the cocktail. The mint and ginger garnishes are also important features, as the little flourishes of sweetness and spice both finish the drink perfectly.

30ml (2 tbsp) Havana Club 3 Year Old Rum
10ml (2 tsp) peach schnapps
Small handful of mint leaves, plus a sprig to garnish
Fever-Tree Naturally Light Tonic Water, to top up
Thin fresh ginger slice, to garnish

Pour all the ingredients except the tonic water in order into a collins or highball glass over ice. Top up with the tonic water. Garnish with a mint sprig and a thin ginger slice.

NEW PINK GIN

This cocktail is a fusion of two classic gin concoctions – Pink Gin and Gin and Tonic – and it pays homage to these two iconic drinks by giving them a modern interpretation. It has been created as a fresh alternative to a G&T, introducing new flavours while still keeping things nice and simple. Always use fresh grapefruit juice; it is an important element to give the zingy, citrus punch that makes this drink so refreshing.

60ml (4 tbsp) Tanqueray No. Ten Gin
60ml (4 tbsp) fresh ruby grapefruit juice
60ml (4 tbsp) Fever-Tree Indian
  Tonic Water
2 dashes of Angostura Bitters
Lemon wedge, to garnish

Pour all the ingredients in order into a highball glass over ice. Stir to mix and add a lemon wedge to garnish.

Angostura Bitters were originally created by a German surgeon in Simón Bolívar's army in Venezuela in the early 19ᵗʰ century. Angostura takes its name from the town it was first distilled in (now Ciudad Bolívar) and the complex recipe remains a closely guarded secret.

SWEET BASIL HEAT

We are surrounded by fresh herbs and produce at Bymark and basil is very prominent during the summer, its invigorating smell permeating the kitchen. This is certainly a summertime cocktail because it's so refreshing, but there's nothing to say that it can't be enjoyed year round. By muddling the basil, the drink achieves a flavour balance that arrives a little at a time – sweet, herby and with a bit of punch at the finish.

4–5 basil leaves, plus a sprig
   to garnish
7.5ml (1½ tsp) limoncello
50ml (2fl oz) Bombay Sapphire East Gin
Squeeze of fresh lemon juice
2 drops of Scrappy's Firewater Bitters,
   or Angostura Bitters
30ml (2 tbsp) Fever-Tree Indian
   Tonic Water

In a mixing glass, muddle the basil leaves with the limoncello. Add the gin and stir well, then pour into a highball glass over ice. Add a squeeze of lemon and the bitters and stir. Add the tonic water. Top up the glass with ice cubes and add a basil sprig to garnish.

MANGO HIGHBALL

Mango is easy to use and adds an interesting summer flavour to drinks. I wanted to create a really simple drink that is easy to recreate at home. This is a long, fruity drink that is crying out for a barbecue and a cloudless day. The fruit gives it a punch-like quality and the dense, sweet mango loves being paired with fresh, sour lime juice. Tonic is used to lighten the drink and add the fizz.

40ml (1¼fl oz) premium vodka

20ml (4 tsp) fresh lime juice

70ml (2½fl oz) mango juice

Fever-Tree Indian Tonic Water, to top up

Mint sprig, to garnish

Pineapple wedge, to garnish

Pour all the ingredients except the tonic water in order into a highball glass over ice. Top up with the tonic water. Garnish with a mint sprig and a wedge of pineapple.

POM POM

This simple cocktail celebrates tequila by not adding too many other ingredients, in order to let the spirit's unique characteristics shine through. Lime is tequila's natural companion and here it's muddled to extract the maximum amount of flavour. The sweet pomegranate sugar and the fizz of the tonic water are all that are needed to create a well-balanced glass. Lime and pomegranate garnish the drink as a way of highlighting these flavours and reminding you of the key components of the Pom Pom. *(Pictured)*

50ml (2fl oz) premium tequila
4 lime wedges, plus a wedge to garnish
10ml (2 tsp) pomegranate sugar or cordial
Fever-Tree Indian Tonic Water, to top up
Pomegranate seeds, to garnish

Muddle the tequila, lime wedges and pomegranate sugar or cordial in the bottom of a highball glass. Fill the glass to the top with ice cubes and then top up with the tonic water. Garnish with a lime wedge and some pomegranate seeds.

Bar: **CANTINA DEL PONTE — LONDON, UK**
Bar person: **SIMONE FRANCINI**

P&T

Pococello is a premium limoncello that was born in Soho and created with lemons from the Amalfi coast. This drink unites London and the Gulf of Naples, garnished with a rosemary sprig and juniper berry to add herbal hints and spiciness to the drink.

35ml (2 generous tbsp) Pococello Limoncello, or other premium limoncello
Fever-Tree Indian Tonic Water, to top up
Rosemary sprig, to garnish
Juniper berry, to garnish

Pour the ingredients into a rocks glass over plenty of ice cubes. Garnish with a rosemary sprig and a juniper berry.

RED SAPPHIRE

The red in the name of this cocktail refers to the Campari, while the sapphire naturally refers to the gin, which forms the base of the drink. We use Bombay Sapphire for its complex flavour that works well with so many ingredients. We have chosen fruit flavours for this cocktail and use fresh lime juice and cranberry bitters to work with the gin and Campari. This is a drink to enjoy with friends any time, any season.

40ml (1¼fl oz) Bombay Sapphire London Dry Gin

20ml (4 tsp) Campari

1 dash of Fee Brothers Cranberry Bitters, or Angostura Bitters

10ml (2 tsp) fresh lime juice

Fever-Tree Indian Tonic Water, to top up

Twist of orange peel, to garnish

Rosemary sprig, to garnish

Pour all the ingredients except the tonic water into a cocktail shaker and shake vigorously. Double-strain into a highball glass filled with ice cubes and top up with the tonic water. Garnish with a twist of orange peel and a sprig of rosemary.

ELMINISTER

Inspired by the classic Clover Club cocktail, this version takes Tanqueray No. Ten Gin and shakes it with the French apéritif Lillet Blanc and a little lime juice and fresh raspberry purée. The colour is incredible and the whole drink fizzes and froths when the tonic is added. Fresh raspberries and cranberries accent the red colour of the drink and add a lightness and freshness, as well as a gorgeous aroma as you lift the glass for the first sip.

30ml (2 tbsp) simple sugar syrup (see page 13)

30g (1oz) crushed raspberries

40ml (1¼fl oz) Tanqueray No. Ten Gin

20ml (4 tsp) Lillet Blanc

20ml (4 tsp) fresh lime juice

1 dash of The Bitter Truth Creole Bitters, or Angostura Bitters

60ml (4 tbsp) Fever-Tree Indian Tonic Water

To garnish

Raspberries

Cranberries

Icing sugar

Mix the sugar syrup and crushed raspberries together well. Put all the ingredients except the tonic water into a Boston shaker with ice and shake vigorously. Open the shaker, add the tonic water and stir. Double-strain the drink into a goblet or wine glass and add a few small ice cubes. Put a few raspberries and cranberries on top of the ice cubes and sprinkle with a little icing sugar to garnish.

OLOROSO SPRITZ

I love making Sbagliati and the nuttiness of oloroso sherries, which combine beautifully with the bitterness of tonic. From the name, it's obvious that the inspiration for this drink came about from wanting to create a recognizable variation on the famous Aperol Spritz. This is a bright, lightly bitter drink in a similar guise to the original: it's sunshine drinking for people who prefer more bitter flavours than a traditional spritz.

25ml (5 tsp) oloroso sherry
25ml (5 tsp) Martini Rosso Vermouth
75ml (5 tbsp) prosecco
25ml (5 tsp) Fever-Tree Indian Tonic Water
Pink grapefruit wedge, to garnish

Pour all the ingredients in order into a wine glass over ice. Garnish with a pink grapefruit wedge.

FORDS RED TEA & TONIC

A Gin and Tonic is one of life's most simple and perfect pleasures and so is a lovely cup of tea: I wanted to combine the two. This is an easy-drinking cocktail, suitable for day- or night-time imbibing. The clean, classic taste of the tonic works incredibly well with rooibos tea and, of course, gin. The tea syrup is really easy to make and worth it in order to enjoy this unusual and refreshing drink. *(Pictured overleaf left)*

Distilled in London, Fords Gin is a blend of juniper, coriander and citrus notes, forming a traditional and well balanced flavour.

50ml (2fl oz) Fords Gin
20ml (4 tsp) rooibos tea syrup (see below)
20ml (4 tsp) fresh lemon juice
Fever-Tree Indian Tonic Water, to top up
Lemon wheel, to garnish
Mint sprig, to garnish

Rooibos tea syrup
450g (1lb) granulated sugar
225ml (8fl oz) warm-brewed rooibos tea

To make the rooibos tea syrup, stir the sugar into the tea until dissolved, then leave to cool at room temperature. This will keep in a sterilized and sealed bottle in a cool, dark place for up to 1 week.

To make the cocktail, add all the ingredients in order to a large highball glass filled with ice cubes. Garnish with a lemon wheel and a mint sprig.

BLACK ROSE

This cocktail captures the essence of the classic Gin and Tonic but takes things a step further with the addition of the delicious blackberry syrup, which is sweet, rich and fruity. It really complements the gin in this drink and the blackberry flavour is intensified by reducing the blackberries with sugar. This refreshing drink is cool, smooth and beautifully hued with the colour of the fruit. It's served in a goblet glass and garnished with a fragrant rosemary sprig. *(Pictured overleaf right)*

50ml (2fl oz) gin
30ml (2 tbsp) blackberry syrup (*see below*)
Lime wheel
Fever-Tree Indian Tonic Water, to top up
Rosemary sprig, to garnish

Blackberry syrup
140g (5oz) blackberries
100g (3½oz) granulated sugar
100ml (3½fl oz) water
zest of 1 lemon
2 thyme sprigs

To make the blackberry syrup, heat the blackberries, sugar and measured water in a saucepan until boiling. Reduce the heat and simmer for 20 minutes. Remove from the heat and add the lemon zest and thyme and leave to steep for 20 minutes. Strain and pour into a sterilized glass bottle. This will keep in the sealed bottle in a cool, dark place for up to 2 weeks.

To make the cocktail, put the gin, syrup and lime wheel into a cocktail shaker. Shake well and muddle. Add ice cubes and shake, then strain into a chilled goblet over ice. Top up with the tonic water and garnish with a rosemary sprig.

Left: **FORDS RED TEA & TONIC**
— *see page 56*
Right: **BLACK ROSE** — *see page 57*

SILK HIGHWAY

I was immensely inspired by the origins of tonic. When British colonies protected their trade routes for exotic spices and imports along the Silk Road, they discovered local tonics in the 19th century, which included Indian quinine. The British added seltzer, sugar and eventually gin to balance the taste and enhance its effects. My cocktail pays homage to history by using London dry gin, Fever-Tree Tonic, fig, citrus and cinnamon to really capture the spirit and flavours of the Silk Road.

2 figs, plus an extra slice to garnish

2 dashes of The Bitter Truth Lemon Bitters, or Angostura Bitters

1 cinnamon stick

15ml (1 tbsp) fresh lemon juice

20ml (4 tsp) demerara or brown sugar syrup (see page 13)

45ml (3 tbsp) Martin Miller's Westbourne Gin

30ml (2 tbsp) Fever-Tree Indian Tonic Water

Cut the figs in half and then muddle in a cocktail shaker. Add the bitters. Rapidly grate the cinnamon stick for 5 seconds into the shaker, then add the lemon juice, sugar syrup and gin. Add ice and shake well. Add the tonic water to the shaker and strain into a collins glass filled with ice cubes. Garnish with a fig slice and the remainder of the cinnamon stick.

FAITH IN PALOMA

The name of the cocktail is a play on the name of the singer Paloma Faith and a tequila-based classic cocktail Paloma. I was looking for a way to introduce people to mezcal in an approachable way and this combination popped into my mind. Mezcal is still relatively unknown as a spirit category – its flavour is similar to tequila with varying degrees of smokiness. In the original drink the bitterness comes from grapefruit, whereas in my creation it is the tonic water that provides this flavour. The drink itself is light, with smoky and bitter notes, but it is also quite floral and easy to drink.

35ml (2 generous tbsp) Ilegal Mezcal Joven
20ml (4 tsp) St-Germain elderflower liqueur
15ml (1 tbsp) fresh lime juice
3 dashes of Peychaud's Bitters
Fever-Tree Indian Tonic Water, or Fever-Tree Naturally Light Tonic Water for an even lighter version, to top up
Pink grapefruit slice, to garnish

Pour all the ingredients except the tonic water into a cocktail shaker. Shake vigorously and strain into a highball glass filled with ice cubes. Top up with the tonic water and garnish with a pink grapefruit slice.

BOURBON & PEAR HIGHBALL

I love pairing sweet ingredients with dry liquors such as sherry, and American bourbon sits perfectly in between the sweetness of Amaretto and the dryness of oloroso sherry. This is a long cocktail that has quite heavy base flavours, yet still manages to end up relatively light and refreshing. This is probably because of the pear juice and the top of tonic water, which provide refreshing elements that balance out the spirits.

30ml (2 tbsp) Buffalo Trace Bourbon

10ml (2 tsp) Disaronno Amaretto

10ml (2 tsp) oloroso sherry

50ml (2fl oz) pear juice

Fever-Tree Naturally Light Tonic Water, to top up

Pear fan (see page 32), to garnish

Raspberry, to garnish

Pour all the ingredients except the tonic water in order into a highball glass over ice cubes, then top up with the tonic water. Garnish with a pear fan with a raspberry on the end.

GINGER

FEVER-TREE GINGER BEER & GINGER ALE

Ginger is probably the world's most cultivated spice and one of the most well known. From the powdered ginger used in baking to the root ginger in the grocery aisle, it's a flavour we all assume we know. It was only when we began to develop our ginger ale and our ginger beer that we realized how wrong we were. Different gingers from around the world differ profoundly in aroma, pungency, piquancy and taste.

VARIETY IS THE SPICE OF LIFE

Perhaps we should not have been surprised. Ginger cultivation goes back at least 5,000 years, and the descendants of those plants grow in a hundred combinations of soils, climates and conditions. It's something you only truly grasp when you're confronted with a cupboard full of ginger samples, from subtle to startling variations on a familiar ginger theme.

Ginger is a flavour enhancer. Just as properly made tonic water allows different gins to shine, so too properly made ginger ale illuminates dark spirits, especially whiskies, while the more robust taste and aroma of ginger beer enliven both vodka and dark rums.

We had gone to meet Alastair and Peter Hitchen, leading flavour experts in the UK,

as a vital step in deciding how we wanted Fever-Tree's ginger to taste. Thanks to Charles's time running Plymouth Gin, we understood that botanical flavours change from cultivar to cultivar and from harvest to harvest, and the need to be able to manage those changes to create a consistent product. Each year at Plymouth Gin, Master Distiller Sean Harrison selects the juniper and other botanicals from a range of batches, micro-distilling them down to blend into the "Plymouth" taste. We now set out to do the same with our ginger.

A FRESH, RICH TWIST ON FAMILIAR GINGER

As we conducted our research we quickly noted that, when rival ginger beers want to trumpet their ginger content, they tended to headline Jamaican ginger as a signal of quality. But actually, a stunning variety of gingers are available, some far more interesting to our noses than Jamaican.

As an aside, we could also taste that the leading ginger ale had virtually no ginger aroma or taste at all. To us, that would create an existential crisis: what is ginger ale without any ginger? We might as well pour brown lemonade into our scotch. So when we sat down with Peter Hitchen and his team, we were very specific. We

What is ginger ale without any ginger?

Fever-tree uses a blend of gingers harvested in Ivory Coast, Nigeria and India.

wanted to find the best-tasting gingers, no matter the cost.

The first ginger we embraced came from Ivory Coast. It smells fresh and green, and its brightness was exactly what we were looking for. Again, we had to make sure we could establish a good relationship with the producers to ensure we could buy it in the quantities we needed, and this time Charles ventured forth to meet its maker.

Ivory Coast is a fascinating country. Despite two civil wars in recent years, it remains, among other things, the world's largest exporter of cocoa. Our ginger producers farm in the heart of cocoa country, west from Abidjan. Here they harvest, press and distil the small, intensely flavoured roots all in the same day in order to achieve a ginger oil of extraordinary freshness. It smells almost citrus-y, like morning dew on a ginger leaf, and its freshness is integral to our ginger style.

Our second ginger comes from Cochin in India. If the Ivory Coast ginger provides the top notes of our blend, the Cochin ginger provides the bass. It has a rich, musky, chocolatey aroma. We visited our suppliers there, too, and, happily surviving the roads, found a family-run business that is completely dedicated to producing only the finest products.

Our third ginger comes from Nigeria. This offers the most familiar ginger scent – the heart of the ginger flavour that we were looking for.

The key advantage to "hand sourcing" ginger like this, quite apart from the adventure (when you find yourself deep in rural Ivory Coast, there is a certain lack of infrastructure: if a cocoa truck should tip over on the road in front of you, which it did, the only way round it is to cut a bypass out of the forest with a machete), is that it gives us control of the ginger from the moment of harvest to the moment we blend our gingers into the drinks, ensuring almost no loss of flavour from the harvest to the final drink. And in the process we came upon a marvellously energetic French septuagenarian, Jacques Touche, who was living again in his beloved Ivory Coast, and who was helping to set up the distillation process on behalf of the owners – another example of drinks bringing like-minded people together.

THE ROOT OF OUR GINGER DRINKS
Ginger beer and ginger ale are fundamentally different. Ginger beer dates back at least as far as the 17th century. It was in its original form a naturally fermented drink – a so-called "small beer", which meant that it typically contained only a little alcohol: just enough to make it safer than water, which back then was often contaminated, but not strong enough to

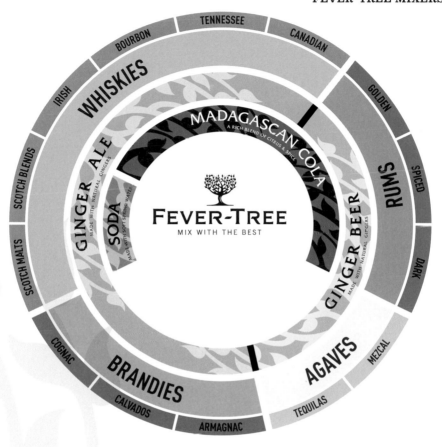

*If a cocoa truck should tip over on the road in front of
you, the only way round it is to cut a bypass out of
the forest with a machete.*

render you insensible. Modern ginger beer is non-alcoholic (unless it says otherwise on the label), and it should remain a brewed product. But it is also one that has become very commoditized. The big companies pull every trick in the book to create the impression of ginger in their drinks without having to use much, if any, ginger at all. For example, some use unappealing sounding ingredients such as "esters of wood resins" to create a cloudy suspension that you might associate with proper ginger beer. But rest assured that at Fever-Tree we use natural ginger root brewed to perfection, and the resultant delicious drink has won awards around the globe.

Ginger ale is unbrewed. It is made by extracting the sparingly soluble ginger oils, the so called "shogaols", and then dissolving them in tiny amounts of alcohol so they will mix with water, diluting and carbonating the resulting liquor. The current form of "dry ginger ale" was created in 1904 by the Canadian chemist John McLaughlin. It is, or should be, a subtle drink that puts ginger's flavour-enhancing qualities at the fore, bringing out the vanillas, oaks or spicy, smoky or peaty notes in dark spirits. And of course, it's also a delicious soft drink option.

ANOTHER TONIC

Quinine is not the only hero ingredient with medicinal benefits. In addition to ginger's charms as a spice, its health uses are extolled in the Indian writings, the *Compendium of Caraka* and the *Compendium of Susruta*, of the 1st and 2nd centuries. The Greek physician Dioscorides, whose work was a standard medical text for 1,500 years, tells us that ginger is a marvellous digestive aid, "warming and softening the stomach". These well-known qualities made it one of the world's most traded spices and its very name tells the story of its travels. The Old English name *gingifer* comes from the Medieval Latin *gingiber*, from the Classical Latin *zingiberi*, which in turn evolves from the Sanskrit word *srngaveram*.

Harvested ginger in Cochin, India.

THE CLASSICS

ULTIMATE MOSCOW MULE

The Moscow Mule (its name referring to the common perception of vodka as a Russian product) became popular during the 1950s in the United States when a vodka craze swept the nation. Vodka remains the country's most popular spirit. *(Pictured right)*

½ a lime, plus a wedge to garnish
50ml (2fl oz) premium vodka
200ml (7fl oz) Fever-Tree Ginger Beer

Fill a copper mug with ice cubes. Squeeze over the lime half, then drop it into the mug. Add the vodka and then the ginger beer. Garnish with a lime wedge.

ULTIMATE RUM & GINGER

The rich and sometimes spicy notes of the finest dark rums pair perfectly with the warmth of the natural ginger that is packed into Fever-Tree Ginger Beer. This makes for one of the most refreshing cocktails around and is very simple to make. *(Pictured left)*

50ml (2fl oz) premium dark rum
200ml (7fl oz) Fever-Tree Ginger Beer
Lime wedge, to garnish
Fresh ginger slice, to garnish

Pour the rum followed by the ginger beer into a highball glass over ice cubes. Garnish with a lime wedge and ginger slice.

ULTIMATE WHISKY & GINGER

A delicious drink for the winter, ginger ale is less fiery than ginger beer but it retains the warming aromas of fresh ginger without overpowering the flavours of your favourite whisky. *(Pictured right)*

25ml (2fl oz) premium whisky
100ml (7fl oz) Fever-Tree Ginger Ale
Fresh ginger slice, to garnish

Add the whisky to a rocks glass filled with ice cubes. Top up with the ginger ale and garnish with a ginger slice.

EL DIABLO

Tequila and lime are natural bedfellows and the El Diablo combines them into a refreshing drink. The sweetness of the crème de cassis balances out the sourness of the lime and the ginger ale adds a spicy flavour to pack a punch into this devilish cocktail. *(Pictured left)*

50ml (2fl oz) premium white tequila
25ml (5 tsp) fresh lime juice
10ml (2 tsp) ginger juice or ginger cordial
10ml (2 tsp) crème de cassis
Fever-Tree Ginger Ale, to top up
Lime wedge, to garnish
Mint sprig, to garnish

Pour all the ingredients except the ginger ale into a cocktail shaker and shake. Strain into a highball glass filled with ice cubes and top up with the ginger ale. Garnish with a lime wedge and mint sprig.

GUNNER

Strictly speaking, bitters are alcoholic but the amount usually used is so tiny that this makes a great virgin cocktail. *(Pictured left)*

1 dash of Angostura Bitters
150ml (5fl oz) Fever-Tree Ginger Ale
150ml (5fl oz) Fever-Tree Ginger Beer
Lime wedge, plus peel to garnish

Fill a collins glass with ice cubes, add the Angostura Bitters, followed by the the ginger ale and ginger beer. Squeeze in the lime wedge, then garnish with the lime peel.

THE BUCK

Buck refers to a family of cocktails using ginger mixers with citrus juice and a base spirit. *(Pictured right)*

50ml (2fl oz) premium gin
15ml (1 tbsp) fresh lemon juice
Fever-Tree Ginger Ale, to top up
Lemon wedge, to garnish

Pour the gin and lemon juice into a collins glass filled with ice cubes and top up with the ginger ale. Stir and simply garnish with a lemon wedge.

ULTIMATE COGNAC & GINGER

Warm ginger combines with the sweet vanilla and fruity notes of cognac to create an elegant and aromatic drink.

50ml (2fl oz) premium cognac
150ml (5fl oz) Fever-Tree Ginger Ale
Twist of lime peel, to garnish

Pour the cognac into a highball glass, fill the glass with ice cubes, then add the ginger ale and garnish with a twist of lime peel.

MILLER MULE

This easy twist on a classic Moscow Mule is delicious, easy to prepare and immensely satisfying; it's a gateway to classic cocktails. The cocktail is named after our bar and uses a Caribbean rum blended with 13 spices, with hints of caramel that sweeten the drink. (Pictured)

2 lime wedges
50ml (2fl oz) The Kraken Black Spiced Rum
Fever-Tree Ginger Beer, to top up

Squeeze over and then drop 1 of the lime wedges into a copper mug or highball glass. Add the rum and some ice cubes. Top up with the ginger beer. Stir gently to combine. Garnish with the remaining lime wedge.

MEXICAN MULE

This is a really simple cocktail that concentrates on the distinctive characteristics of Ocho Reposado tequila. I didn't want to add too many other ingredients that might hide its unique flavour but, at the same time, I wanted to create a cocktail rather than a simple mixed drink. Fresh lime juice is the natural companion to tequila and a central flavour in Mexican culture, but the drink isn't too sharp or sour, as the ginger beer balances out these flavours.

50ml (2fl oz) Tequila Ocho Reposado
15ml (1 tbsp) fresh lime juice
Fever-Tree Ginger Beer, to top up

To garnish
Mint sprig
Twist of lime peel
Dash of Angostura Bitters

Add all the ingredients in order to a highball glass filled with ice cubes. Garnish with a mint sprig, a twist of lime peel and a dash of Angostura Bitters.

AMANACER FIZZ

A fizz is a mixed drink and a variation on the older sours cocktail family. Its defining features are an acidic juice (such as lemon or lime) and carbonated water. The fizz became widely popular in America between 1900 and the 1940s. Known as a hometown speciality of New Orleans, the Gin Fizz was so popular that bars would employ teams of bartenders to take turns shaking the drinks. A Gin Fizz is the best-known cocktail in the fizz family. It contains gin, lemon juice and sugar, which are shaken with ice, poured into a tumbler and topped with carbonated water.

45ml (3 tbsp) Barsol Pisco
15ml (1 tbsp) Aperol
15ml (1 tbsp) Gancia Bianco Vermouth
20ml (4 tsp) fresh pink grapefruit juice
10ml (2 tsp) simple sugar syrup (*see* page 13)
100ml (3½fl oz) Fever-Tree Ginger Beer
Dehydrated lime slice, to garnish
Dehydrated papaya slice, to garnish

Pour all the ingredients except the ginger beer into a cocktail shaker and shake well. Double-strain into a goblet over a chunk of ice. Top with the ginger beer and garnish with dehydrated lime and papaya slices.

EL BURRO CATALAN

Every fine drinking establishment needs a Moscow Mule these days – be it a local drinking den or a fine-dining restaurant bar, and this drink won the prestigious Tales of the Cocktail 2016 Competition. Its name comes from the Burro, an icon in Catalan culture, and it brings flair to a legendary classic. Sherry gives it a lovely dry finish, while the spice in the ginger beer wakes up and readies the palate. It's perfect for my bar, as nearly everyone is there to snack on our Barcelona-inspired tapas.

50ml (2fl oz) Absolut Elyx Vodka
25ml (5 tsp) La Cigarrera Manzanilla
    Sherry, or other crisp manzanilla
15ml (1 tbsp) Starvation Alley Fresh
    Pressed Cranberry Juice, or other
    100 per cent cranberry juice (no sugar,
    water or preservatives added)
15ml (1 tbsp) natural cane sugar
15ml (1 tbsp) fresh lemon juice
2 dashes of Angostura Bitters
75ml (5 tbsp) Fever-Tree Ginger Beer
Twist of lemon peel, to garnish
Dried or fresh cranberries, to garnish

Pour all the ingredients except the ginger beer into a cocktail shaker and shake. Double-strain into a copper mug over crushed ice, then add the ginger beer and top up with pebble ice cubes or more crushed ice. Twist the lemon peel over the drink to release the oils. Add 2 short straws and garnish with skewered cranberries wrapped with the expressed lemon peel.

Bar: NAO STEAKHOUSE – TORONTO, CANADA
Bar person: BRANDON MOUNSEY

SUMMER FIZZ

A spin on a classic Gin Fizz, the Summer Fizz is a refreshing cocktail to be enjoyed after a long, hot day in the sun. Fresh aromatic ingredients, such as mint and cucumber, balanced with just the right amount of citrus, give the drink an invigorating and refreshing taste very similar to a Tom Collins. Served with large cubes of ice and topped off with Fever-Tree Ginger Ale, this is the perfect summer drink. *(Pictured)*

1 slice of cucumber, cut into 4 pieces
8 mint leaves, plus a sprig to garnish
30ml (2 tbsp) fresh lime juice
45ml (3 tbsp) gin, preferably Bombay Sapphire
150ml (5fl oz) Fever-Tree Ginger Ale

Muddle the cucumber, mint leaves and lime juice in a Boston shaker. Add ice and the gin and shake for 20 seconds. Strain into a collins glass filled with ice cubes and top up with the ginger ale. Garnish with a mint sprig.

Bar: MANHATTAN BAR – HILDESHEIM, GERMANY
Bar person: NILS BOESE

MEISTERHAFT

This is a take on the classic tiki drink, with the Jägermeister adding herbal spiciness to the fruity base. There's more complexity here than in the original version, with crème de cassis adding sweetness and the ginger adding heat and spice. It's served with plenty of crushed ice and should be drunk through a straw to ensure a chilled drink with every sip.

20ml (4 tsp) Jägermeister
30ml (2 tbsp) reposado tequila
10ml (2 tsp) Giffard Crème de Cassis de Bourgogne, or other crème de cassis
Fever-Tree Ginger Ale, to top up
2 lime wedges, to garnish

Pour all the ingredients except the ginger ale into a double rocks glass over crushed ice. Top up with the ginger ale, garnish with lime wedges and serve with a straw.

BOMBAY SQUALL

The Bombay Squall is a subtle twist on the Dark & Stormy cocktail, with the added hint of cardamom, which is a prominent spice in Indian cooking. In the Bahamas, rum is a frequently used spirit: using Plantation Original Dark Rum rather than a Jamaican dark rum it gives the drink a bit more mellowness and elegance. The rum itself has notes of clove and banana that add to the cocktail's complexity. I wanted to create something that allows you to conjure up memories of the classic while tasting something completely new. This is the ideal drink to enjoy with the sand between your toes while watching the sun going down over the ocean!

45ml (3 tbsp) Plantation Original Dark Rum, or other dark rum
4 dashes of Scrappy's Cardamom Bitters, or cardamom-infused rum (see below)
15ml (1 tbsp) fresh lime juice
Fever-Tree Ginger Beer, to top up
Lime wedge, to garnish

Cardamom-infused rum
Cardamom pods, whole
Dark rum

To make the cardamom-infused rum add the cardamom pods (1 pod for every 100ml/3½fl oz of rum) and the rum to a bottle and leave to infuse for 2–3 hours, shaking occasionally. The infused rum will keep in the sealed bottle in a cool, dark place for up to 1 week. Strain before use to remove the pods.

To make the cocktail, fill a highball glass with ice cubes. Add the rum, bitters or cardamom-infused rum, and lime juice, then top up with the ginger beer and lightly stir to incorporate. Garnish with a lime wedge for those who may want to squeeze a little more tartness into their drink.

BASTA POCO

Basta Poco is a simple, three-ingredient cocktail that was first created for an Italian trattoria with the same name. I wanted to create an alternative to the very popular Aperol Spritz – a drink that was less bitter but had some kind of kick at the same time. In this instance, the kick comes from the spicy ginger ale, which is offset by the bubbles from the Spumante, and it's a delicious combination of flavours. This makes a perfect, low-alcohol apéritif that also works very well as a nightlife party drink – perfect after a hard day as a toast to living life to the full.

50ml (2fl oz) Fever-Tree Ginger Ale
50ml (2fl oz) Cocchi Americano, or any
    white vermouth
50ml (2fl oz) TotoCorde Alta Langa DOCG
    or other good-quality Spumante,
    or Champagne
Twist of orange peel, to garnish

Add all the ingredients over a few big ice cubes in a large Burgundy glass. Garnish by twisting a piece of orange peel to release the oils onto the drink.

GOLDEN MOMENT

This drink has been created to enjoy in a quiet pause after a busy day. Calvados and Amaretto are the base spirits and the addition of fresh lemon juice and orange bitters ensure the dominant flavours shine. The ginger ale adds a sweet and spicy note that tops up the tumbler to make this a long drink. The final touch is a cherry garnish.

45ml (3 tbsp) Calvados, Single Cask Collection
20ml (4 tsp) Disaronno Amaretto
20ml (4 tsp) fresh lemon juice
2 dashes of Angostura Orange Bitters
60ml (4 tbsp) Fever-Tree Ginger Ale
Cocktail cherry, to garnish

Pour all the ingredients except the ginger ale into a cocktail shaker. Shake, then double-strain into a big glass tumbler over ice. Top up with the ginger ale and garnish with a cherry.

The Disaronno recipe dates back to the renaissance where the artist Bernardino Luini was commissioned to paint a fresco in Saronno. He used a beautiful local innkeeper as his model, who prepared the artist an incredible delicate, aromatic liqueur as a gesture of gratitude.

GINGER JULEP

Ginger is one of my favourite ingredients – tasty, spicy, inexpensive and healthy – and it works well with so many other ingredients. It adds a kick to this julep variation, which works well as both an apéritif and a digestif. The drink isn't too strong so can be sipped throughout the evening – make sure the straw is very short so that your nose is just above the glass and each sip is accompanied by the fresh aroma of the mint garnish. This cocktail pairs particularly well with fish and seafood.

12–15 mint leaves, plus sprigs to garnish
50ml (2fl oz) Angostura White Oak Rum
20ml (4 tsp) St-Germain elderflower
   liqueur
40ml (1¼fl oz) fresh pink grapefruit juice
Fresh lime juice, to taste
40ml (1¼fl oz) Fever-Tree Ginger Beer

Lightly muddle the mint leaves in the bottom of a julep cup or highball glass filled with ice, then add all the other ingredients and stir until the cup is frozen outside. Crush the mint sprigs lightly on the back of your hand, then add to the cup or glass to garnish. Serve with 2 short straws.

Bar: RUBY — COPENHAGEN, DENMARK
Bar person: JEPPE NOTHLEV

RUBY WINTER CUP

The Ruby Winter Cup is a wintry version of a Pimm's Cup. It's a really simple cocktail with just a few ingredients and the warmth of the ginger ale helps to add a seasonal element to the drink. We use Ron Zacapa, which is a premium rum from Guatemala. The quality of the rum is all important, as this is the key ingredient in the cocktail.

40ml (1¼fl oz) Ron Zacapa Rum
20ml (4 tsp) Pimm's No. 1 Cup
120ml (4fl oz) Fever-Tree Ginger Ale

To garnish
Choose from cinnamon, star anise, mint leaves, cloves, orange zest, redcurrants, icing sugar…and whatever else you can think of!

Pour all the ingredients into a wine glass over ice cubes. Garnish lavishly with seasonal winter ingredients.

NON-ALCOHOLIC BASIL FIZZ

If you're not drinking alcohol, there's no need to miss out on great drinks. This complex cocktail might be missing a spirit base but the depth of flavours that are present in the other ingredients more than make up for its absence. Heady basil syrup, sharp citrus juice and spicy ginger beer all vie for attention in the glass, while the egg white binds everything together.

60ml (4 tbsp) fresh citrus juice
40ml (1¼fl oz) basil syrup (muddle a handful of basil leaves with simple sugar syrup, *see* page 13)
20ml (4 tsp) egg white
3 basil leaves
Fever-Tree Ginger Beer, to top up

Add all the ingredients except the ginger beer to a cocktail shaker with ice. Shake well and strain into a highball glass over ice. Top up with the ginger beer.

The term "basil", has its origins in the word "basileus", meaning "king" in Greek.

MELONCHOLY

We live in a region where huge watermelons can be found for sale on every street corner. Watermelon is a very forgiving ingredient, as it will work well with most other ingredients. Personally, I like to combine it with earthy flavours to mellow out the sweetness. The Meloncholy is a very thirst-quenching drink that is best enjoyed over crushed ice when you're relaxing at the weekend.

45ml (3 tbsp) Herradura Reposado Tequila
45ml (3 tbsp) fresh watermelon juice
25ml (5 tsp) fresh lime juice
10ml (2 tsp) cinnamon syrup (either shop-bought or homemade, see below)
2 dashes of Angostura Bitters
45ml (1½fl oz) Fever-Tree Ginger Beer
Watermelon slice, to garnish
Grated fresh cinnamon, to garnish

Cinnamon syrup
200g (7oz) granulated sugar
100ml (3½fl oz) water
5 cinnamon sticks, crushed

To make the cinnamon syrup, add the sugar and measured water to a saucepan and bring to the boil, stirring constantly. Add the cinnamon sticks and remove from the heat. Leave to cool before straining into a sterilized glass jar. The syrup will keep for up to 3 months in the refrigerator.

To make the cocktail, shake all the ingredients except the ginger beer together vigorously, then strain into a Mason or Kilner jar filled with ice cubes and top up with the ginger beer. Garnish with a watermelon slice and cinnamon gratings. Alternatively, blend all of the ingredients in a blender with crushed ice, pour into a margarita glass over crushed ice, grab your umbrella straw and imagine hanging out on the beach with us.

PANACEA

"Panacea" is a Latin word that derives from Greek and means a cure-all for illness and diseases – this is what we believe our Panacea will do for you. If not, it will make you feel better than when you first arrived. We use the drink today as an alternative to the notorious Dark & Stormy cocktail, giving people the opportunity to try something new that we created here in the bar.

60ml (4 tbsp) Ron Zacapa 23 Rum
20ml (4 tsp) fresh lemon juice
10ml (2 tsp) honey
2 dashes of Angostura Bitters
2 dashes of orange bitters
1 drop of Élixir Végétal de la Grande-
    Chartreuse, or green Chartreuse
1 dash of egg white
Fever-Tree Ginger Beer, to top up
Fresh ginger slice, to garnish

Pour all the ingredients except the ginger beer into a cocktail shaker and shake well, then strain into a highball glass filled with ice cubes. Top up with the ginger beer and garnish with a ginger slice.

GINGER FIZZ

This cocktail has a distinct ginger flavour and belongs in the fizz cocktail family. Its inspiration comes from the classic Singapore Sling cocktail, with a few additions to liven up the fruitiness of the drink. The cocktail offers the perfect combination of Tanqueray No. Ten Gin and Luxardo cherry liqueur with the addition of fresh lime juice, pineapple and ginger beer – sweet, gingery and sparkling. The cherry garnish elevates the cherry element in the drink and gives it a fun flourish.

50ml (2fl oz) Tanqueray No. Ten Gin
10ml (2 tsp) Luxardo cherry liqueur
30ml (2 tbsp) fresh lime juice
60ml (4 tbsp) pineapple juice
50ml (2fl oz) Fever-Tree Ginger Beer
Fresh ginger fan (see page 32), to garnish
Fresh cherry, to garnish

Add all the ingredients except the ginger beer to a Boston shaker. Fill it with ice cubes and shake vigorously. Add the ginger beer to the shaker and stir. Strain the drink into a tall sling glass and add crushed ice. To garnish, create a small hill of crushed ice, then add a sliced ginger fan with a fresh cherry on top of the ice.

Luxardo boasts a rich history of complex cherry liqueur recipes dating back to 1821. Their liqueurs have an intense flavour of marasca juice, with some liqueurs taking as many as four years to produce.

SEAFARER'S MULE

Not one for the faint-hearted, this strong, flavoursome combination of spiced rum and white rum will warm you up on a chilly evening. The name comes from the Sailor Jerry rum that is used in the drink – a punchy rum packed with flavours and herbs, with distinct notes of vanilla and cinnamon. The raspberry syrup adds fruitiness and sweetness, while the ginger beer gives the drink a fizzy finish.

3–4 raspberries

10ml (2 tsp) simple sugar syrup (*see* page 13)

20ml (4 tsp) fresh lemon juice

30ml (2 tbsp) Sailor Jerry Spiced Rum

10ml (2 tsp) Clairin Sajous Rhum Agricole, or any cachaça

Fever-Tree Ginger Beer, to top up

3 dashes of Angostura Bitters, to garnish

Muddle the raspberries and sugar syrup in a mixing glass. Add the raspberry mixture with all the remaining ingredients, except the ginger beer, in order to a highball glass filled with ice cubes. Top up with the ginger beer and float the bitters on top.

ET VOILÀ

Et Voilà is a tribute to the relationship between French people and people abroad. Almost everyone knows a few French phrases; *et voilà* is one of them.

During a selection for a bar contest in France, I wanted to use Calle 23, made in Mexico by a French woman. The ingredients are carefully built around the tequila. The St-Germain adds floral sweetness to balance its strength, while the agave syrup complements it. Sweet and citrus flavours, and a hint of heat, come from lemon juice and ginger ale.

50ml (2fl oz) Calle 23 Blanco Tequila
25ml (5 tsp) St-Germain elderflower liqueur
10ml (2 tsp) agave syrup (see page 13)
15ml (1 tbsp) fresh lemon juice
Sprig of fresh coriander
1 egg white
15ml (1 tbsp) Fever-Tree Ginger Ale
Twist of lemon peel, to garnish

Pour all the ingredients except the ginger ale into a cocktail shaker and shake; use a Hawthorn strainer in order to have a nice foam on the top, if possible. Double-strain into a wine glass or goblet, then add the ginger ale. Squeeze over the lemon peel to release the oils and then drop it onto the glass to garnish.

FRENCH RUBIS MULE

Rotonda Bistro specializes in creating low-alcohol cocktails and, as such, any spirits used in the drinks must be less than 21 per cent ABV. This drink is our version of the classic Moscow Mule, which is a legendary cocktail but obviously high in alcohol content. So, we set about designing a version of the drink in the French style. At 20 per cent ABV, St-Germain elderflower liqueur fits the bill perfectly and this is complemented by fruity Chambord, lime juice and ginger beer.

The cocktail is served in a Mason jar, which means it gets lots of attention in the bar and is perfect for those who love the classic Moscow Mule but are looking for something fresher and lighter.

15ml (1 tbsp) fresh lime juice
30ml (2 tbsp) St-Germain elderflower liqueur
15ml (1 tbsp) Chambord raspberry liqueur
3 slices of lime
Fever-Tree Ginger Beer, to top up
Pieces of dehydrated lime (see page 13), to garnish (optional)
Piece of fresh ginger, cut into small strings, to garnish (optional)

Add crushed ice to a Mason or Kilner jar. Add the fresh lime juice, followed by the St-Germain, Chambord and lime slices. Top up with the ginger beer. Garnish with pieces of dehydrated lime and fresh ginger cut into small strings, if liked, and serve with paper straws.

CHULLACHAQUI

I constantly look to nature for inspiration for my drinks and particularly like including different varieties of fruit. This drink shows off the sweet, summery flavour of pineapple, which works really well with gin, and just enough absinthe to add character. Bitter orange offsets the sweetness, while the spicy notes of the ginger beer add the final flavour element. If you need help ordering this drink at the bar, it's pronounced "choo-ya-chá-key".

45ml (3 tbsp) gin, preferably herbal

45ml (3 tbsp) pineapple juice

4 dashes of absinthe

5ml (1 tsp) bitter orange juice (Amazonian lemon), or lemon juice

45ml (3 tbsp) Fever-Tree Ginger Beer

Dehydrated pineapple and bitter orange slices, or any dehydrated citrus fruit, to garnish

Pour all the ingredients except the ginger beer into a cocktail shaker and shake, then pour into a rocks glass over ice and add the ginger beer. Garnish with dehydrated pineapple and bitter orange slices.

ROOT 56

This simple Jägermeister cocktail emphasizes the incredible spices and herbs that are blended in the German digestif. Lime juice is included for its sour, citrus notes and we top up with the ginger ale for heat and sweetness. The cucumber garnish keeps the drink fresh and light with a definite summer vibe.

40ml (1¼fl oz) Jägermeister
10ml (2 tsp) lime juice
Fever-Tree Ginger Ale, to top up
Cucumber slice, to garnish

Add the Jägermeister and juice to a tall glass over ice. Top up with the ginger ale, garnish with a cucumber slice and serve with a straw.

LA HISTORIA

This fresh and fun cocktail is the perfect start to an evening out with family and friends. Rum and lemon make natural partners, while sweetness and spiciness are added with the orange juice and ginger ale. The cocktail is fairly light in alcohol content so can be enjoyed by those who love spirit-based drinks but are looking for something they can sip all evening.

40ml (1¼fl oz) Angostura 7 Year Old Rum
10ml (2 tsp) fresh lemon juice
30ml (2 tbsp) simple sugar syrup (*see* page 13)
2 dashes of Angostura Bitters
10ml (2 tsp) fresh orange juice
Fever-Tree Ginger Ale, to top up
Twist of orange peel, to garnish
Mint sprig, to garnish

Pour all the ingredients except the ginger ale into a cocktail shaker and shake. Pour into a julep cup and top up with the ginger ale. Garnish with a twist of orange peel and a mint sprig.

THE DON CANTON

This cocktail is named The Don Canton as a reference to the two spirits that we use in it – Don Julio Reposado Tequila and Domaine de Canton ginger liqueur. I wanted to create a tequila cocktail that included ginger beer and I chose this aged tequila, as it holds its own against the spicy notes of the ginger. The agave syrup works with the tequila, while the lemon grass garnish adds a sweet lemon note at the end – the longer this stays in the drink the stronger the flavour will be.

45ml (3 tbsp) Don Julio Reposado Tequila
15ml (1 tbsp) Domaine de Canton, or any
   ginger liqueur
20ml (4 tsp) fresh lime juice
5ml (1 tsp) agave syrup (see page 13)
30ml (2 tbsp) Fever-Tree Ginger Beer

To garnish
Lemon grass
Lime wedge
Fresh ginger slice

Pour all the ingredients except the ginger beer into a cocktail shaker and shake to mix. Strain and pour over ice cubes into a tall or highball glass. Add the ginger beer and some crushed ice, then garnish with lemon grass, lime and ginger.

BEETROOT FIZZ

Rum, citrus, honey and beetroot might sound like an unusual collection of ingredients in a cocktail but they actually work incredibly well together once assembled in the glass. I love looking around the kitchen for new and interesting combinations of ingredients, as well as innovative ways to present and garnish cocktails. Here, I use dehydrated beetroot and rosemary to finish the drink.

50ml (2fl oz) Havana Club 7 Year Old Rum
35ml (2 generous tbsp) any fresh citrus juice
30ml (2 tbsp) honey
25ml (5 tsp) beetroot juice
20ml (4 tsp) egg white
Fever-Tree Ginger Beer, to top up
Dehydrated beetroot slice, to garnish
Rosemary sprig, to garnish

Add all the ingredients except the ginger beer to a cocktail shaker with ice. Shake well and strain into a highball glass over ice. Top up with the ginger beer and garnish with a beetroot slice and rosemary sprig.

CONTINENTAL STORM

If you're familiar with the Dark & Stormy cocktail, then you'll love this fresh new variation on the classic. Like its predecessor, the Continental Storm is a long drink based around the blended white rum Plantation 3 Stars. To this we add a little grenadine, which imparts both flavour and colour to the drink, and the delicate infusion of rosewater – just enough to have a sense of the flavour without overpowering the drink. Ginger beer is the mixer and the spice and heat adds another dimension to the drink.

5ml (1 tsp) grenadine
50ml (2fl oz) Plantation 3 Stars Artisanal Rum
3 drops of rosewater
100ml (3½fl oz) Fever-Tree Ginger Beer
Lime wedge, to garnish

Pour the grenadine, rum, rosewater and half the ginger beer into a short glass or mug over ice and stir gently. Top up with the rest of the ginger beer and garnish with a lime wedge.

STARRY NIGHT

This cocktail celebrates Genever, which is the juniper-flavoured liqueur from Holland that is also known as Dutch gin. Here, it is combined with other floral and fruity ingredients – apricot liqueur, lemon juice, apple juice and honey – for a delightfully fruity drink with a summery freshness. The ingredients are shaken, then strained into a sling glass to ensure clarity, and an apple fan garnish makes it clear that fruit is the star of this pretty cocktail. *(Pictured)*

35ml (2 generous tbsp) Genever
15ml (1 tbsp) apricot brandy or liqueur
20ml (4 tsp) fresh lemon juice
20ml (4 tsp) pressed apple juice
10ml (2 tsp) acacia honey
Fever-Tree Ginger Ale, to top up
Apple fan (see page 32), to garnish

Pour all the ingredients except the ginger ale into a cocktail shaker and shake. Strain into a sling glass over ice and top up with the ginger ale. Garnish with an apple fan.

MI VIDA

I really enjoy the smoky characteristics of mezcal and wanted a variation on the Moscow Mule. I kept the freshly squeezed lime but have used agave syrup as the sugar component, as well as passion fruit purée. As you sip this cocktail, you'll first experience the spice from the ginger beer and the mezcal, followed by a subtle sweetness from the passion fruit. Finally, the sour lime juice helps to bring everything together.

45ml (3 tbsp) Vida Mezcal
20ml (4 tsp) fresh lime juice
20ml (4 tsp) agave syrup (see page 13)
30ml (2 tbsp) passion fruit purée
Fever-Tree Ginger Beer, to top up
Large mint sprig, to garnish

Pour all the ingredients except the ginger beer into a cocktail shaker with ice. Shake well, then fine-strain into a rocks glass filled with ice cubes. Top up with the ginger beer and garnish with mint in the centre.

CREOLE COLLINS

The Creole Collins is inspired by the culture of New Orleans and its most famous drink, the Sazerac. I was looking for a way to prolong the enjoyment of the Sazerac – it's so delicious that it's easy to drink too quickly. So, I created the Creole Collins, which is a longer drink that should be savoured slowly. It has plenty of herbal notes, with a citrus finish and a touch of spice.

40ml (1¼fl oz) Hennessy VSOP
2 dashes of Absinthe
4 dashes of Peychaud's or Angostura
  Bitters
2 pieces of lemon peel
100ml (3½fl oz) Fever-Tree Ginger Ale

Put all the ingredients except the ginger ale into a highball glass filled with ice cubes and stir until chilled. Top up with the ginger ale.

MAGNIFICENT MULE

This is a Chicago-style mule; its name is a play on the Magnificent Mile. The inspiration is a desire to create traditional cocktails with a bit of a twist, in this case a spin on a Moscow Mule but made with Koval Bourbon instead of the traditional vodka. The lemonade and ginger beer add a lightness to the drink, making it perfect for easy summer sipping. The key here is good-quality mixers, as these make up a large part of the cocktail.

45ml (3 tbsp) Koval Bourbon
50ml (2fl oz) Fever-Tree Premium
  Lemonade
50ml (2fl oz) Fever-Tree Ginger Beer
Lemon wedge, to garnish

Pour all the ingredients in order into a highball glass filled with ice cubes. Garnish with a lemon wedge.

APPLE OF MY EYE

I love the combination of apple and ginger for a light, fruity, sweet yet spicy drink. This cocktail was inspired by visits to London and can be enjoyed day or night because of its refreshing taste. Fruit is a definite theme here, with the cider brandy sharing the glass with cranberry juice and citrus juice. The drink is mixed and then topped with a good dash of spicy ginger beer. A simple lime wheel is all that's required in terms of garnish – let the drink speak for itself.

40ml (1¼fl oz) Somerset Cider Brandy, or Calvados
50ml (2fl oz) cranberry juice
20ml (4 tsp) fresh lime juice
50ml (2fl oz) fresh citron juice
Fever-Tree Ginger Beer, to top up
Lime wheel, to garnish

Pour the brandy or Calvados and juices into a cocktail shaker and shake. Pour into a highball glass over ice and top up with the ginger beer. Garnish with a lime wheel.

CHERISH THE DEVIL

This was created entirely by accident, by pouring cherry liqueur instead of cassis into an El Diablo. I was pleasantly surprised to discover that it tasted even better than the original. Although tequila and cherry are rarely paired, they are natural partners in the cocktail glass. And, when you add the lime juice and ginger ale, the result is incredible. *(Pictured right)*

20ml (4 tsp) tequila
20ml (4 tsp) cherry liqueur
20ml (4 tsp) fresh lime juice
80ml (5 tbsp) Fever-Tree Ginger Ale
Lime slice, to garnish

Add all the ingredients except the ginger ale to a highball glass over ice. Top up with the ginger ale and garnish with a lime slice.

RUM & GO

The idea behind this cocktail was to try and introduce a new way to enjoy rum. Here we have created a refreshing drink that includes a touch of cinnamon to complement the rum and add another dimension to the spicy ginger ale. Orange peel and cinnamon are warm, fragrant garnishes that bring all the elements of the drink together. This is a long drink that should be slowly savoured to really appreciate the diverse range of ingredients.

15ml (1 tbsp) cinnamon syrup (*see* page 95)
7.5ml (1½ tsp) fresh lemon juice
7.5ml (1½ tsp) simple sugar syrup (*see* page 13)
60ml (4 tbsp) Plantation 3 Stars Rum
150ml (5fl oz) Fever-Tree Ginger Ale

To garnish
2 cinnamon sticks
Twist of orange peel
Mint sprig

Add all the ingredients except the ginger ale in order to a highball glass over ice. Top up with the ginger ale and garnish with the cinnamon, orange peel and mint sprig.

PICCADILLY COLLINS

This cocktail is called the Piccadilly Collins, as that's where I was working when the inspiration kicked in. Also, I wanted to maintain a cultural approach to the name of the drink. The idea was to create a Collins using ingredients that represent British culture but also come together to form the perfect mix when combined with gin. The drink is refreshing, enticing and delightful but, above all, surprising and, overall, remarkably delicious. There's so much going on in the glass but it's all about the choice of the ingredients and what they can create when combined harmoniously together.

25ml (5 tsp) cucumber juice (see below)
50ml (2fl oz) Hendrick's Gin
25ml (5 tsp) fresh lemon juice
15ml (1 tbsp) St-Germain elderflower liqueur
15ml (1 tbsp) simple sugar syrup (see page 13)
2.5-cm (1-inch) rosemary sprig
125ml (4fl oz) Fever-Tree Ginger Ale

To garnish
Strip of cucumber peel
Olive
Rosemary sprig

Cucumber juice (yield varies)
1 cucumber, peeled and chopped

To make the cucumber juice, blitz the cucumber in a powerful food processor for 1 minute. Strain and discard the pulp.

To make the cocktail, add all the ingredients except the ginger ale to a cocktail shaker and shake together well. Strain into a highball glass filled with ice cubes. Top up with the ginger ale and garnish with the cucumber peel twirled around the olive and rosemary sprig, and secured with a cocktail stick.

GINGER STORM

Ginger Storm was given its name because of the intense flavour in the cocktail, particularly from the ginger beer. The mix, with the dry curaçao, is like a flavour explosion when you take the first sip. The lemon juice and bitters make this a deliciously sour drink, with a hint of sweetness added from the dash of ginger beer. Warmed coffee beans and rosemary make unusual garnishes but ensure that this drink is perfect for winter evenings.

50ml (2fl oz) Plantation 3 Stars Artisanal Rum

25ml (5 tsp) fresh lemon juice

25ml (5 tsp) Pierre Ferrand Dry Curaçao, or Grand Marnier

3 dashes of The Bitter Truth Jerry Thomas' Own Decanter Bitters, or Angostura Bitters

10ml (2 tsp) Fever-Tree Ginger Beer

Rosemary sprig, to garnish

Warmed coffee beans, to garnish

Mix all the ingredients except the ginger beer in a cocktail shaker, then add the ginger beer and mix with a bar spoon. Pour into a rocks glass over crushed ice. Garnish with a rosemary sprig and some warmed coffee beans.

BLUEBERRY BUCK

The blueberry and sage infusion is what makes this drink extra special so it's worth taking the time to prepare it for a batch of drinks. Once the infusion is ready, the cocktail is pretty much good to go, with just a top-up of ginger beer to complement the existing flavours. Crushed ice dilutes the drink sufficiently and sage and lemon garnishes are the finishing touches.

45ml (3 tbsp) blueberry & sage infusion (*see below*)
Splash of fresh lime juice
125ml (4fl oz) Fever-Tree Ginger Beer
Lemon slice, to garnish
Sage leaf, to garnish

Blueberry & sage infusion
600g (1lb 5oz) fresh blueberries
25g (1oz) chopped sage
800g (1lb 12oz) granulated sugar
550ml (18½fl oz) filtered water
1.5 litres (3 pints) Banyan Reserve Vodka, or other vodka

To make the blueberry and sage infusion, muddle the blueberries, sage and sugar in a large Mason or Kilner jar until the sugar is dissolved. Seal and place in the refrigerator for 24–36 hours. Add the filtered water to the jar and shake well. Pour all the contents of the jar into a strainer and press the syrup through, discarding the liquid and reserving the solids. Add the vodka to the solids in a sterilized glass bottle and leave to infuse for up to 3 days. Strain and store the final syrup in a sealed sterilized bottle in a cool, dark place for up to 2 weeks.

To make the cocktail, pour all the ingredients over crushed ice into a highball glass or julep cup. Garnish with a lemon slice and sage leaf.

APRICOT SPLASH

If you're more used to seeing Jägermeister served as a single shot then this drink will be a pleasant introduction to its use in cocktails. Combined with the glorious Sipsmith gin, this is a refreshing drink packed with botanicals, herbs and spices. We included the apricot jam for sweetness and to highlight the other flavours. Spicy ginger ale adds another dimension to this long drink, while the rosemary garnish brings everything together.

40ml (1¼fl oz) Jägermeister
20ml (4 tsp) Sipsmith Dry Gin
30ml (2 tbsp) fresh lime juice
30g (1oz) apricot jam
Fever-Tree Ginger Ale, to top up
Rosemary sprig, to garnish

Shake all the ingredients except the ginger ale in a cocktail shaker filled with ice cubes, then strain into a tall or collins glass filled with ice cubes. Top up with the ginger ale. Garnish with a rosemary sprig.

GOLDEN MULE

You don't often see a cocktail that includes saffron but its vibrant colour and rich flavour work perfectly here as an infusion for quality Russian Standard vodka. The spicy theme doesn't end with saffron: cardamom pods and ginger are muddled together to create an exotic backdrop for the other ingredients. The cocktail is strained to achieve just the right balance of flavours and to ensure no single ingredient overpowers the others.

1 slice of fresh ginger

3 cardamom pods

50ml (2fl oz) saffron infused Russian Standard Gold Vodka (add 1 tbsp saffron to the vodka bottle, shake and leave to infuse for 2 days)

20ml (4 tsp) fresh lime juice

15ml (1 tbsp) simple sugar syrup (see page 13)

Fever-Tree Ginger Beer, to top up

Lime wheel, or edible gold flakes, to garnish

Muddle the ginger and cardamom pods in a cocktail shaker. Add the rest of the ingredients except the ginger beer. Shake, then strain into a highball glass or copper cup. Fill the cup with crushed ice, then top up with the ginger beer. Garnish with a lime wheel or edible gold flakes sprinkled over.

LEKKERLEKKER

At The Pharmacy we love working with chefs to create new pairings and combinations. We get together and it's like a reunion of a band. Everybody has creative input and new flavours are created. I came up with this cocktail – which is a tribute to everybody who works in hospitality, from chefs to bartenders – to go with fresh seafood. It's an easy sipper that can be enjoyed with a group of friends on a sociable Saturday night but also on the beach after a long day of relaxing. It's complex in flavour but easy on the palate.

5 slices of cucumber, chopped, plus
   2 triangles to garnish
20ml (4 tsp) Ketel One Vodka
30ml (2 tbsp) Filliers Grain Genever
30ml (2 tbsp) fresh lemon juice
20ml (4 tsp) dill syrup (see below)
Fever-Tree Ginger Beer, to top up

Dill syrup (makes 500ml/18fl oz)
25g (1oz) dill, finely chopped
500ml (18fl oz) simple sugar syrup (see
   page 13)

To make the dill syrup, infuse the dill in the sugar syrup for 24 hours. Pour through a strainer to use. This will keep in a steralized botter in the refrigerator for up to a week.

To make the cocktail, muddle the cucumber in the base of a cocktail shaker. Add the rest of the ingredients except the ginger beer, shake and then strain into a tall glass. Top up with the ginger beer and garnish with cucumber triangles.

FRUITS & FLOWERS

FEVER-TREE ELDERFLOWER TONIC, SICILIAN LEMON TONIC & SICILIAN LEMONADE

Come the middle of June, strange things happen in the Gloucestershire countryside. It is the elderflower harvest and people drop everything when the time is right to pick the flowers; it is a part of their annual routine and has been for generations. It's a small business, but the advantage to us is that the flowers are so fresh.

FROM ST-GERMAIN TO GLOUCESTERSHIRE

Our flavoured tonics came about because of the enormous growth and diversity we had seen in gin. The variation in styles and flavour profiles led us to create different types of tonic to go with them. Some gins are floral, some citrus-driven, others more intensely flavoured with juniper, and we noticed that bartenders were mixing the more floral gins with St-Germain. Why not introduce an elderflower tonic to go with them?

As ever, we wanted to find the ultimate elderflower. Usually, elderflowers are dried before the oils are extracted and distilled. But as we had learned with ginger, the brightest, freshest flavours come when the product is processed as soon after harvesting as possible. So we set out to find

the elderflower equivalent of our Ivory Coast ginger. We did not have to travel far.

The Gloucestershire elderflower picking season is short. It will be done in as little as two weeks and the flowers are processed almost immediately. As a result, they create an elderflower flavour that is unique. The oils made from dried flowers lack a fresh immediacy; their aroma feels as though it is missing something. This is a vital realization for what we are trying to achieve with our mixers.

THE PUREST EXPRESSION OF FLAVOUR

The sensual experience of drinking needs to combine a number of stimuli for it to be satisfying. The first is sight. Does the drink look good? For us, the drink should look natural to look good. So many of our competitors need to use colourings and other tricks for their drinks to seem natural. Ours already are.

The second and third are smell and taste. As you raise your glass to your mouth, you cannot help but smell what's in it. The olfactory system receives signals through both your nose and your open mouth. And

The brightest, freshest flavours come when the product is processed as soon after harvesting as possible.

Tim joins in the elderflower harvesting in rural Gloucestershire.

we know that taste as a sense works on the five key elements of sweet, salt, bitter, sour and umami. Thus our perception of flavour derives from a harmonic balance of both taste and smell. The natural elderflower and lemon oils in their respective tonics are there to make sure that the aroma delivers the purest expression we can create of the flavour we want in the drink.

REDEEMING BITTER LEMON

We take the same approach to the lemon in our lemon tonic and our lemonade. Lemon tonic is our answer to the drink formerly known as bitter lemon. It is a fantastic mixer that has been in decline for years, a direct consequence we believe of its being unloved and degraded by its main producers. As ever, we set out to find the best lemon flavour we could.

We found it in lemons grown in the richly fertile soils around Mount Etna in Sicily. As beautiful as the tiny lemon groves there are, what fascinated us was the process by which the lemon oil was harvested. It's called sfumatrice extraction. The lemons are cut in half and then, a half at a time, the lemon skin is rolled in such a way that it presses free the oil, in much the same way as releasing a little lemon zest in your kitchen by running your thumb nail across the skin of an unwaxed fruit. That little mist of oil that sprays out: that's what we want and collect.

It's a very unusual process. More commonly, lemons are run down a shaking table with little rasps that rip everything – the natural wax, fine oils and the thicker oils – out of the lemon skin. Of course, it's much less expensive and thus widely used.

Our lemon-growing hosts, having shown us the fruits and the various methods of extracting the oils available, then asked us to smell a selection of different lemon oils to choose the one we liked. Of course, one oil was notably different. It is the single most lemony thing either of us had ever smelled. It was also five times the price of everything else on the table. In fact, the only other people who use it are perfumers.

ONLY THE BEST WILL DO

This brings up one of the key things that makes Fever-Tree different from everybody else making mixers. In the 14 years and counting that we have been crafting these mixers, three of the flavour houses we have worked with explain to us that we are alone. No one else had ever asked them to start a project based purely on using the finest ingredients available.

We can state absolutely that our tonics contain the purest source of natural quinine available, the lemon oils we add have no equal in the drinks industry, the elderflowers are as fresh as it is possible to obtain. Indeed, all our ingredients are as high quality as it is possible to obtain.

Super-fresh lemons are transported for sfumatrice extraction in Sicily.

THE CLASSICS

ULTIMATE ELDERFLOWER G&T

**The delicate, sweet elderflower
perfectly balances the soft bitterness
of the quinine, providing a summery,
refreshing floral twist on the classic Gin
and Tonic.**

50ml (2fl oz) premium gin
200ml (7fl oz) Fever-Tree Elderflower
    Tonic Water
Twist of orange peel, to garnish

*Fill a highball glass with ice cubes. Pour
in the gin, followed by the tonic water and
garnish with a twist of orange.*

NAUGHTY ST CLEMENT'S

**To make a virgin version of this cocktail,
leave out the spirits and add a dash of
Angostura Bitters.** *(Pictured)*

25ml (5 tsp) premium vodka
25ml (5 tsp) Grand Marnier
75ml (5 tbsp) fresh orange juice
75ml (5 tbsp) Fever-Tree Sicilian Lemon
    Tonic
Orange slice, to garnish
Lemon slice, to garnish

*Fill a highball glass with ice cubes. Pour
in the vodka, Grand Marnier and orange
juice, followed by the tonic. Garnish with
orange and lemon slices.*

SLOE GIN & LEMON

Sloe Gin is deliciously sweet with rich notes of plum and red berries. Combining this fruity sweetness with the bitter notes found in Fever-Tree Lemon Tonic Water makes for a perfectly balanced and refreshing long drink. This is a perfect daytime cocktail and ideal for those looking for something sweeter than an ordinary Gin and Tonic. *(Pictured)*

50ml (2fl oz) premium sloe gin
100–150ml (3½–5fl oz) Fever-Tree Sicilian
   Lemon Tonic
Lemon slice, to garnish

Measure the gin into a highball glass. Add enough ice cubes to fill the glass, then add the tonic to taste. Garnish with a lemon slice.

WHISKY & LEMON

Sicilian Lemonade provides the perfect balance between sweetness and acidity, allowing the original flavour and mouth-feel of your favourite whisky to be enjoyed unaltered.

50ml (2fl oz) premium whisky
150ml (5fl oz) Fever-Tree Sicilian
   Lemonade
Lemon slice, to garnish

Add all the ingredients to a highball glass over ice and garnish with a lemon slice.

LEMON BERRY FEVER

The mild flavour of vodka allows the delicious fruity blend of lemon and blackcurrant to take centre stage in this colourful summer tipple. *(Pictured left)*

25ml (1fl oz) premium vodka
1 dash of blackcurrant liqueur
100ml (3½fl oz) Fever-Tree Sicilian
    Lemonade
Twist of lemon peel, or lemon wedge,
    to garnish

Fill a rocks glass with at least 4 big ice cubes. Pour over the vodka, then the blackcurrant liqueur. Add the lemonade and garnish with a twist of lemon peel or a lemon wedge.

COINTREAU & LEMON

The highest-quality Sicilian lemon oils bring a soft, subtle lemon note to complement the sweetness of Cointreau. *(Pictured right)*

50ml (2fl oz) Cointreau
200ml (7fl oz) Fever-Tree Sicilian
    Lemon Tonic
Lemon wheel, to garnish

Add all the ingredients to a goblet over ice and garnish with a lemon wheel.

QUIYAYA

The idea behind this cocktail came from the long, slender shape of our country, Chile. From the Atacama Desert in the north, to the vast expanse of Patagonia in the south, the indigenous plants and flowers have helped to shape the cuisine of the country and can be found in many dishes and drinks. Here, we have used ulmo honey, Chilean papaya and the malva leaf to create a unique drink that really epitomizes Chile. Of course, there's also a good splash of Pisco.

70ml (2½fl oz) Pisco Waqar D.O
20ml (4 tsp) ulmo or other honey
20ml (4 tsp) fresh papaya juice
200ml (7fl oz) Fever-Tree Elderflower
   Tonic Water

To garnish
1 malva leaf, or any edible decorative
   leaf (optional)
1 star anise
Fresh ginger slice
Chilean papaya slice, or regular papaya

Pour all the ingredients into a rocks glass filled with ice cubes. Stir gently, then garnish with an edible leaf if using, star anise, fresh ginger and a papaya slice.

THE GRANITA FIZZ

The Granita Fizz, a twist on the classic Gin Fizz, is named after the famous lemon sorbet dessert from Sicily. We served this recipe at the King Charles II pop-up bar in Rotterdam in the summer – it's very refreshing and can be served as an apéritif or digestif.

30ml (2 tbsp) Bobby's Gin

20ml (4 tsp) Cocchi Americano, or any white vermouth

25ml (5 tsp) fresh lemon juice

15ml (1 tbsp) simple sugar syrup (*see* page 13)

1 egg white

Fever-Tree Sicilian Lemonade, to top up

Twist of lemon peel, to garnish

Mint sprig, to garnish

Add all the ingredients except the lemonade to a cocktail shaker and shake. Add ice cubes to the cocktail shaker, then strain into a collins glass filled with ice cubes. Top up with the lemonade and garnish with a twist of lemon peel and a mint sprig.

Bobby's is named after the founder's grandfather who enjoyed infusing Dutch genever (a rich malted grain spirit flavoured with juniper) with Indonesian spices. Both of these influences can be tasted in Bobby's Gin.

LEMONADE CUP

Lemonade is a classic ingredient in apéritifs because of its sweetness combined with the fresh, citrus flavour. This drink offers a variation for Pimm's Cup fans – it is light and refreshing with plenty of fresh fruit and served with orange peel rubbed around the glass rim and plenty of ice. Keep it seasonal with your choice of fruit – we particularly like strawberries, raspberries and mint.

A mix of seasonal fruit and herbs, we used
  2 strawberries, sliced, 2 raspberries,
  2 blueberries and lime wedges
50ml (2fl oz) Sipsmith Summer Cup, or
  Pimm's No. 1 Cup
2 dashes of orange bitters
200ml (7fl oz) Fever-Tree Sicilian
  Lemonade
Twist of orange peel, to garnish
Mint sprig, to garnish

Put all the fruit into a wine glass, then add the Summer Cup or Pimm's and the bitters. Add plenty of ice cubes, then pour in the lemonade. Finally, run the orange peel around the rim of the glass before dropping it into the drink. Garnish the cocktail with a mint sprig.

SOUTHSIDE

Steam Hellsinki is themed around Victorian England and steampunk and we specialize in Gin and Tonic and cocktails that feature gin as the main ingredient. The Southside is a personal favourite of mine and I've been making it throughout my 16 years working in the industry. I love the fact that big-time gangsters drank this cocktail during Prohibition in the speakeasies of Chicago.

35ml (2 generous tbsp) fresh lemon juice

5ml (1 tsp) simple sugar syrup (*see* page 13)

45ml (3 tbsp) Bloom Premium London Dry Gin

5ml (1 tsp) Grand Marnier

5 mint leaves, plus a sprig to garnish

Fever-Tree Elderflower Tonic Water, to top up

Long strip of grapefruit peel, to garnish

Pour all the ingredients except the tonic water into a cocktail shaker filled with ice. Shake, then double-strain into a chilled coupette. Gently top up with the tonic water using a bar spoon. Garnish with a long strip of grapefruit peel and a mint sprig.

Bloom gin is the brain-child of Joanne Moore, one of the world's first female master distillers. It accentuates many floral notes including chamomile and honeysuckle.

JAPANESE BLOSSOM

Spring sakura blossom is incredibly beautiful and it's the most famous blossom in the world. I used this gift from nature as an inspiration so I could share the Japanese culture with everyone. This drink should be served in a highball glass and enjoyed chilled, so you experience the feeling of spring in Japan. The low alcohol content means the drink can be drunk by anyone, at any time.

45ml (3 tbsp) white rum

35ml (2 generous tbsp) elderflower liqueur

20ml (4 tsp) fresh lemon juice

30ml (2 tbsp) pineapple juice

10ml (2 tsp) honey

1 shiso (perilla) leaf (optional)

Fever-Tree Elderflower Tonic Water,
   to top up

Pour all the ingredients except the tonic water into a cocktail shaker and shake hard. Strain into a chilled highball glass filled with ice cubes. Top up with the tonic water and garnish with a shiso leaf, if liked.

TORPEDO BLU

This drink is named after the 1960s Italian song and the ingredients take you on a journey from Mexico to the Italian Alps, combining flavours from the sea and the mountains. Elderflower Tonic Water and Italian blueberry liqueur create a light, fruity backdrop for the piquancy of the tequila and fresh lime juice. This is a chilled, tall drink that should be slowly savoured on a sunny evening.

50ml (2fl oz) El Jimador Blanco Tequila
20ml (4 tsp) Italian blueberry liqueur, or Chambord raspberry liqueur, or crème de cassis
5ml (1 tsp) simple sugar syrup (*see* page 13)
30ml (2 tbsp) fresh lime juice
Fever-Tree Elderflower Tonic Water, to top up
Mint sprig, to garnish
Fresh blueberries, to garnish

Pour all the ingredients except the tonic water into a Boston shaker and shake well. Strain into a collins or highball glass full of ice cubes, then top up with the tonic water. Garnish with a mint sprig and fresh blueberries.

Jimador is the name given to the worker who chops the Agave plant to make tequila.

SAKE TONIC

At Pakta restaurant, Peruvian and Japanese ingredients and dishes fuse to create an eclectic menu inspired by Nikkei cuisine. The bar also embraces this fusion with drinks, using a wide variety of everyday and unusual ingredients. Sake is the most popular drink at the restaurant and here we combine it with aromatic elderflower to create a fresh and fruity cocktail that can be enjoyed either with food or as an apéritif.

2–3 dried apricots
50ml (2fl oz) sake
25ml (5 tsp) vodka
15ml (1 tbsp) elderflower liqueur
200ml (7fl oz) Fever-Tree Elderflower
　　Tonic Water
Twist of orange peel, to garnish

Cut the apricots into thin slices and add them to a tall glass, such as a collins glass. Pour in the sake, followed by the vodka and elderflower liqueur. Add ice cubes and the tonic water. Finally, add the orange peel twist to garnish, running it around the rim of the glass before dropping it into the drink.

BITTERSWEET

This is a very simple but delicious pairing of sweet vermouth and tangy bitter lemon so we use the best ingredients. Dolin Rouge vermouth has a lovely balance of bitter and sweet. The lemon peel that finishes the cocktail highlights the citrus flavours and helps to bring all the elements together. *(Pictured)*

50ml (2fl oz) Dolin Rouge Vermouth de Chambéry, or other sweet vermouth
50ml (2fl oz) Fever-Tree Sicilian Lemon Tonic
Twist of lemon peel, to garnish

Pour both ingredients into a rocks glass over ice. Garnish with a twist of lemon peel.

CAROUSEL COLLINS

The "carousel" refers to the kaleidoscope of flavours in this fruity drink with sour overtones. Macchu Pisco is a grape brandy that's commonly used in Pisco Sours but it works well here, complementing the splash of sweet Madeira. We finish the drink with a flaming spray of absinthe for a touch of theatre in what is already an unusual and impressive drink but at home we would recommend just adding a dash of absinthe.

50ml (2fl oz) Macchu Pisco
30ml (2 tbsp) fresh grapefruit juice
20ml (4 tsp) fresh lemon juice
10ml (2 tsp) sweet, 10-year-old Madeira
1 egg white
Fever-Tree Sicilian Lemon Tonic, to top up
5 drops of The Bitter Truth Creole Bitters, or Angostura Bitters, to garnish
1 dash of absinthe (preferably Mansinthe), to garnish

Shake the first 5 ingredients with ice in a cocktail shaker. Strain and shake again. Pour into a sling glass and top up with the tonic. Garnish with bitters and absinthe.

ELDER ROOTS

Most of my cocktail names involve a pun or a play on words. In this case, it's obvious with "elder" coming from the elderflower tonic and "roots" from the raw beetroot juice. At first glance, these ingredients – along with the vermouth and rhubarb bitters – might seem like an odd combination, but I love to experiment with ingredients that are less commonly used in drinks; savoury herbs, vegetables and spices all add a whole new element to cocktails. Plus, the beet juice gives this particular cocktail an amazing pink hue. Elder Roots is ideally served as an apéritif-style drink that opens your palate for all that is yet to come.

45ml (3 tbsp) The Botanist Gin, or other botanical gin
15ml (1 tbsp) Carpano Antica Formula, or any red vermouth
30ml (2 tbsp) red beetroot juice
25ml (5 tsp) fresh lemon juice
2 dashes of Fee Brothers Rhubarb Bitters, other rhubarb bitters, or Angostura Bitters
45ml (3 tbsp) Fever-Tree Elderflower Tonic Water
Large dehydrated red beetroot slice, to garnish
Large twist of lemon peel, to garnish

Pour all the ingredients except the tonic water into a cocktail shaker filled with plenty of ice cubes. Shake hard, then strain into a tall collins glass with a single spear of ice and top up gently with the tonic water. For the garnish, combine a dehydrated beetroot slice with a twist of lemon peel for aroma.

LIAISON VERTE

Just a few ingredients create a floral drink that includes a rosemary and basil garnish for an unusual finish. Polish potato vodka is the base ingredient and this works really well with the piquant green apple syrup and sweet elderflower tonic. A popular cocktail in the bar, it embodies the quirky personality of the 25hours Hotel.

50ml (2fl oz) Chopin Potato Vodka

20ml (4 tsp) fresh lemon juice

40ml (1¼fl oz) Monin Green Apple Syrup, or fresh apple juice

Fever-Tree Elderflower Tonic Water, to top up

Rosemary sprig, to garnish

Basil sprig, to garnish

Pour all the ingredients except the tonic water into a cocktail shaker. Shake well, then double-strain into a highball glass over ice. Top up with the tonic water. Garnish with rosemary and basil sprigs.

The production of Chopin Potato Vodka is done in small batches. Just 3kg (7lb) of potatoes are used to make every bottle.

CITRUSY DROP

At Cantina del Ponte, we recommend enjoying this citrus cocktail as a digestif. The base spirits are Pococello Limoncello – produced by Chase Distillery – and vodka, which are paired with lime cordial and fresh lemon juice for a real zesty hit. Bitter lemon completes the refreshing sour notes of this summery drink, which is strained to ensure clarity and smoothness.

25ml (5 tsp) Pococello Limoncello, or other premium limoncello
10ml (2 tsp) lime cordial
40ml (1¼fl oz) vodka
20ml (4 tsp) fresh lemon juice
Fever-Tree Sicilian Lemon Tonic, to top up
Twist of lime peel, to garnish

Pour all the ingredients except the tonic into a cocktail shaker or mixing glass and stir gently. Strain into a martini glass, top up with the tonic and garnish with a twist of lime peel.

RISING SUN FIZZ

A good helping of the Scottish favourite, Johnnie Walker, would seem to indicate that this is a very British cocktail. However, the whisky is joined in the glass with a generous helping of Japanese yuzu seasoning – a tart condiment that's made from the yuzu citrus fruit. Another cocktail that uses egg white to add depth, the fizz in the name comes from the addition of a lemonade top – sweet, sour, bitter and salt combine to create a rounded drink.

50ml (2fl oz) Johnnie Walker Gold Label Reserve Whisky
15ml (1 tbsp) Yuzu Citrus Seasoning, or fresh lemon juice and a pinch of sea salt
5ml (1 tsp) fresh lemon juice
5ml (1 tsp) simple sugar syrup (see page 13)
30ml (2 tbsp) egg white
Fever-Tree Sicilian Lemonade, to top up
Lemon wedge, to garnish

Add all the ingredients except the lemonade to a cocktail shaker with ice and shake well. Strain into a rocks glass over ice and top up with the lemonade. Garnish with a lemon wedge.

John Walker, the founder of the whisky, was in fact teetotal.

L'ORANGERIE

A beautiful summer drink that is ideal for fans of Scotch whisky. It errs on the dry side and has a long citrus finish, inspired by the classic Lynchburg Lemonade. This cocktail is refreshing and citrusy without losing sight of the star ingredient – the Glenmorangie – or diluting its distinctive characteristics. The citrus theme is continued with the garnish, which is a simple rough slice of orange peel.

45ml (3 tbsp) Glenmorangie Original
    Single Malt Scotch Whisky
15ml (1 tbsp) Mandarine Napoléon,
    or 20ml (4 tsp) Cointreau
15ml (1 tbsp) fresh lemon juice
Fever-Tree Sicilian Lemonade, to top up
Large twist of orange peel, to garnish

Shake all the ingredients except the lemonade in a cocktail shaker. Strain into a highball glass over ice cubes. Top up with the lemonade and garnish with a twist of orange peel.

AMALFI-ICE

This is a zesty lemon cocktail that is inspired by sorbet. This refreshingly light, iced amuse-bouche is often seen on the dining tables of Italy, especially at banquets, when sorbet is traditionally served between the fish and meat dishes, to refresh the palate. This drink serves the same purpose, with Pococello and creamy vanilla ice cream offering chilled refreshment with a sweet overtone. The lemonade adds another hit of citrus and helps to create a frothy top to the drink.

35ml (2 generous tbsp) Pococello Limoncello, or other premium limoncello
15ml (1 tbsp) vodka
1 scoop of vanilla ice cream
Fever-Tree Sicilian Lemonade, to top up
Twist of lemon peel, to garnish

Pour all the ingredients except the lemonade into a cocktail shaker and shake well. Pour into a coupette glass and garnish with a twist of lemon peel.

UNDER THE HOST

There's a lot going on in this refreshing long drink. It focuses on elderflower flavours, pairing St-Germain liqueur with elderflower tonic water. Sugar syrup and egg white add sweetness and depth, while the addition of Cocchi Americano softens the drink. This Italian apéritif wine produced in Amalfi is low in alcohol – a good thing as there's a decent helping of gin in the drink.

45ml (3 tbsp) Dorothy Parker Gin

15ml (1 tbsp) St-Germain elderflower liqueur

10ml (2 tsp) Cocchi Americano, or dry white vermouth

10ml (2 tsp) fresh lemon juice

5ml (1 tsp) simple sugar syrup (*see* page 13)

20ml (4 tsp) egg white

Fever-Tree Elderflower Tonic Water, to top up

Twist of lemon peel, to garnish

Add all the ingredients except the tonic water to a cocktail shaker with ice and shake well. Strain into a rocks glass over ice and top up with the tonic water. Garnish with a twist of lemon peel.

THE ELDERFLOWER COOLER

The idea behind this cocktail was to make a summertime drink using elderflower tonic water. The raspberries add vibrancy to the flavour and colour of the drink, while the lemon juice imparts an important citrus element. This is complemented by the sweet freshness of the mint sprig. Elderflower is a quintessentially British summer flavour so this is a perfect tipple for al fresco dining, plus it looks impressive despite being very easy to make at home.

50ml (2fl oz) Plymouth Gin
25ml (5 tsp) fresh lemon juice
4 raspberries
Fever-Tree Elderflower Tonic Water, to top up
Mint sprig, to garnish

Pour the Plymouth Gin and lemon juice into a rocks glass. Add the raspberries and muddle. Fill the glass with ice cubes and top up with the tonic water to taste. Stir gently, bringing the ingredients from the bottom up to the top. Garnish with a mint sprig.

HEDGEROW TONIC

Combining floral elderflower with fruity spirits, this drink is a celebration of summer foraging.

25ml (5 tsp) premium gin
10ml (2 tsp) Cointreau
10ml (2 tsp) Chambord
125ml (4fl oz) Fever-Tree Elderflower Tonic Water
Raspberry and blackberry, to garnish

Add all the ingredients in order to a highball glass over ice. Garnish with the fruit.

NUEVA PALOMA

This cocktail should be served in a highball glass with plenty of ice to keep the drink chilled while it's savoured. Tequila is the star of the show here and Ocho Blanco is a 100 per cent agave tequila. The addition of agave nectar helps to accentuate the flavour, while the freshly squeezed pink grapefruit juice adds both citrus notes and a touch of sweetness. A final flourish of bitter and sweet comes from the top of bitter lemon. It's a simple collection of ingredients that have been carefully calculated to create the perfect balance.

Sea salt, to frost the glass rim
50ml (2fl oz) Tequila Ocho Blanco
15ml (1 tbsp) fresh lime juice
10ml (2 tsp) agave nectar
50ml (2fl oz) fresh pink grapefruit juice
Fever-Tree Sicilian Lemon Tonic, to top up
Pink grapefruit wedge, to garnish
Mint sprig, to garnish (optional)

Frost the rim of a highball glass with the sea salt (see page 12).

Fill the glass with ice cubes and pour in all the ingredients except the tonic. Top up with the tonic. Garnish with a pink grapefruit wedge and a mint sprig, if liked.

GREEN DAY

This is the perfect drink for when you feel like sipping something light, fresh and summery but not too sweet. Most people know cachaça, thanks to the popular cocktail Caipirinha, and I wanted to create a lighter version of it, using herbs and fruit. I've chosen cucumber and mint but lemon thyme, basil, rosemary, fennel or dill would work equally well and this drink allows for experimentation more than others. The flavour is light and crisp and will be enhanced by whatever herb you choose to use. Likewise, the apple juice can be replaced by pineapple juice, which would give the drink a tropical twist.

1 strip of cucumber peel, plus a cucumber slice to garnish
6–8 mint leaves, plus a sprig to garnish
15ml (1 tbsp) fresh lime juice
30ml (2 tbsp) fresh apple juice, or pineapple juice for a tropical twist
50ml (2fl oz) Abelha Organic Cachaça, or Yaguara Organic Cachaça
Fever-Tree Sicilian Lemonade, to top up

Put the cucumber peel, mint leaves, lime and apple juices and cachaça into a cocktail shaker. Shake vigorously and double-strain into a highball or sling glass filled with ice cubes. Top up with the lemonade, stir gently and garnish with a cucumber slice and mint sprig.

Bar: 56 NORTH – EDINBURGH, UK

Bar person: JAMES SUTHERLAND

APPLE GARDEN

This cocktail uses a stunning foraged botanical Scottish gin. It has natural affinity with red apple – hence the name. We have over 250 gins in the bar and have always aimed to stock the very best Scottish varieties. We love the guys at Caorunn, and the Speyside area of Scotland is simply one of the most amazing areas in the UK for scenery, as well as gin, so it was a natural fit for us. *(Pictured)*

50ml (2fl oz) Caorunn Gin

1 tsp finely grated lemon zest

3–4 red apple wedges

Fever-Tree Elderflower Tonic Water,
    to top up

Mint sprig, to garnish

Add all the ingredients except the tonic water to a large goblet or wine glass with ice. Top up with the tonic water and garnish with a mint sprig.

Bar: QUALITY MEATS – NEW YORK, USA

Bar person: BRYAN SCHNEIDER

CHINATO SPRITZ

Barolo Chinato is a wonderfully complex aromatized wine. Barolo wine is infused with a blend of herbs, including cinchona, which pairs perfectly with the bitter lemon of the tonic water. This is a perfect apéritif – a simple, long drink that can be enjoyed during the day or the evening. It's ideal for those who enjoy wine but are looking for something a little lighter than a classic spirit-based cocktail.

90ml (3fl oz) Cocchi Barolo Chinato, or any
    barolo chinato (we use Marolo Barolo
    Chinato)

90ml (3fl oz) Fever-Tree Sicilian Lemon
    Tonic

Long twist of lemon peel, to garnish

Fresh seasonal fruits, to garnish

Pour all the ingredients into a wine glass filled with ice cubes. Garnish with a long twist of lemon peel and whatever fresh seasonal fruits are available.

BEES JEEVES, BEES!

At Steam Hellsinki we concentrate on G&Ts and classic gin cocktails with only the best fresh ingredients. When guests are not familiar with classic cocktails, or even gin, I often recommend them a Tom Collins, a "tuned up" gin sour or this. This is one of the best cocktails I have ever made and is light, but heavy enough to feel like a real drink. *(Pictured overleaf right)*

20ml (4 tsp) set natural honey

30ml (2 tbsp) fresh lemon juice

10ml (2 tsp) hot water

10ml (2 tsp) green or yellow Chartreuse

40ml (1¼fl oz) Hayman's Old Tom Gin

1 dash of Angostura Orange Bitters

Fever-Tree Sicilian Lemonade, to top up

Stir the honey with the hot water until completely dissolved. Pour all the ingredients except the lemonade into a cocktail shaker with ice. Shake, then strain into a collins or highball glass filled with ice cubes. Top up with the lemonade.

"Old Tom gin" is a style that dates back to the Gin Craze of the 1700s, and traditionally is sweeter than other gins. Plenty of (probably apocryphal) tales surround its history, but one story notes that, while the government was cracking down on gin production in the early 18th century, a sign picturing a black cat (or "Old Tom") would mark where one could purchase illicit gin.

DESIRE LAMP

The base for this cocktail is the Dutch vodka Ketel One. It was created when a Dutch customer mentioned their preference for vodka with an elderflower mixer. Here, we've added lemon juice and St-Germain – the lemon juice adds a sour note and the elderflower liqueur picks up the floral flavour. In the bar, this cocktail is served in a brass pot with lemon verbena and dry-ice flowers; at home you could use a tall glass and a twist of lemon. (Pictured overleaf centre)

50ml (2fl oz) Ketel One Vodka
200ml (7fl oz) Fever-Tree Elderflower
    Tonic Water
15ml (1 tbsp) fresh lemon juice
5ml (1 tsp) St-Germain elderflower liqueur
Lemon verbena sprig, or a twist of lemon
    peel, to garnish

Pour all the ingredients into a Boston shaker and shake. Strain into a tall glass over ice and add a sprig of lemon verbena or a twist of lemon peel to garnish

DUCKY SPRITZ

The spritz style of cocktail is so simple to make and the perfect drink for a summer day. Vodka and lemon are natural partners, while the addition of sauvignon blanc and elderflower tonic adds sweetness and lightness to the drink. Citrus garnishes complement the key flavours but you can also add berries for a seasonal flourish to finish this classy cocktail. (Pictured overleaf left)

50ml (2fl oz) Aylesbury Duck Vodka
20ml (4 tsp) fresh lemon juice
50ml (2fl oz) sauvignon blanc
Fever-Tree Elderflower Tonic Water, to
    top up
Lemon and orange slices, or seasonal
    berries, to garnish

Pour the ingredients in order into a large Burgundy glass over ice. Garnish with citrus slices or seasonal berries – or both.

Left: **DUCKY SPRITZ**
  – see page 173
Centre: **DESIRE LAMP**
  – see page 173
Right: **BEES JEEVES, BEES!**
  – see page 172

FALSO SPRITZ

This is our take on the classic Venetian cocktail called the Spritz. We've adapted it to include some typical ingredients from Peru, the star being Pisco Torontel – the brandy produced from the Torontel grape. The drink is inspired by hot Peruvian summers, so needs to be served extra chilled with the sweet elderflower and sour grapefruit juice quenching your thirst.

45ml (3 tbsp) Pisco Torontel, or other pisco
30ml (2 tbsp) Aperol
45ml (3 tbsp) fresh grapefruit juice
Fever-Tree Elderflower Tonic Water, to top up
Basil sprig, to garnish
Twist of grapefruit peel, to garnish

Pour all the ingredients except the tonic water into a chilled tumbler or highball glass over ice. Top up with the tonic water to taste, and garnish with a basil sprig and twist of grapefruit peel.

HERBS & SPICES

FEVER-TREE MADAGASCAN COLA, AROMATIC
& MEDITERRANEAN TONIC WATERS

People think that vanilla is the most boring flavour in the world. But nothing could be further from the truth. Its apparent ubiquity notwithstanding (which is largely down to the use of vanilla essence, which as a general rule has no real vanilla in it), vanilla is very, very hard to produce.

VANILLA IS ANYTHING BUT...

The vanilla plant originally came from Mexico. It is now grown from China to Turkey, but the only bee able to pollinate it lives...in Mexico. Thus every vanilla vine grown anywhere else has to be pollinated by hand. To complicate matters each vine will have many flowers, which open at different times, and each of these will have to be pollinated in order to produce the vanilla pod we know. Using a specially hooked piece of bamboo or needle the farmer (or his wife) can painstakingly pollinate each flower. They may farm an acre, in which case they are unable to leave the land for a few weeks until it is all done.

Once they have done this successfully, they now have to wait for the bean pod to develop and grow, becoming what is then reckoned to be the second-most expensive spice in the world, beaten only by saffron.

So valued is it that a farmer and his family also sleep with their vanilla crop as it grows to prevent it being stolen. Some of them even mark their pods with their own small stamp or trademark to discourage theft.

The green vanilla pods must then be picked at exactly the right time as they start to develop brown pigmentation, before they are sold to the co-operative, from where they will be blanched, sun-dried and sold. Some of this, from Madagascar, will end up in our cola.

BATTLING COLA'S DEMONS

At the time of writing, cola is the newest addition to our range. It is a drink that brings with it a set of distinct challenges and the primary one is the consumer's preconceived idea of what a cola is.

Coca-Cola was invented in Atlanta, Georgia in 1886. It remains the most widely consumed single soft drink in the world and its success ensured that imitators quickly followed, including Pepsi Cola in 1898. Further less well-known versions appeared from there, all around the world.

However, we are possibly the first to create a cola formulation specifically as a mixer

*If kola nuts are the feet of the flavour profile, grounding it,
then vanilla forms its spine.*

for alcoholic drinks. Several of the spirits companies we work with in rum and whisky had mentioned how the acid in standard colas (phosphoric acid – the one that dissolves teeth) is too aggressive and "kills" the spirit taste, and all commercial colas were far too sweet for many adult tastes. So this became a challenge that we could work on in line with the rest of the drinks in the Fever-Tree family: achieving great taste and mouthfeel to support rums and a selection of whiskies.

Vanilla crops are so precious that often whole families will sleep alongside their crops to deter thieves.

Charles inspects the sun-drying vanilla pods.

A COMPLEX BLEND

One of the curious things about cola is that the ingredient from which it takes its name, the kola nut, does not drive the drink's core flavour. Instead, it imparts an earthiness and a bitterness that underlies it. If kola nuts are the feet of the flavour profile, grounding it, then vanilla forms its spine. The flavour we created is a complex blend of 20 different herbs and spices, sourced from all over the world and including Jamaican allspice and Indonesian cassia. And crucially, we provide the necessary acidity for a cola using citric acid, giving a much softer effect as a mixer. This gives the cola complexity and profile and, while some of the spices shine through as individuals – which can particularly complement rum and the smokier whiskies – if we removed any one element, the drink as a whole would no longer work.

CAPTURING ANGOSTURA'S AROMA

With the creation of our cola, we locked into a very specific flavour story. But with our Aromatic Tonic – a much simpler drink to conceive – we were able to give our imaginations a little more of a free rein.

Angostura trees are native to South America, where their bark has long been prized for both its flavour and medicinal properties (it is believed in small doses to settle the stomach, and in larger ones to work as a purgative). As an ingredient, the bark brings a bitter flavour, in addition to adding colour, both of which we like. Naval records in the British Library told us that sailors were using angostura bark to flavour their tonic from at least the early 1800s. But what we were really after was its unique aroma, which we wanted to use as a foil for the richer, more juniper-driven gins on the market. Here the bitter angostura bark flavour helps to provide a baritone note to the tonic alongside the quinine's deep bass. Its sweet nose accents a scent of allspice berries, rounding out the top notes and bringing the rest of the tonic's aromatics to the fore.

ETERNAL SUMMER

If our Aromatic Tonic speaks to the Caribbean, our Mediterranean Tonic returns us to thoughts of European summers. Gin and tonic has always been popular in southern Europe, especially in Spain. And, once again, the plurality of gin styles on the market led us toward thinking about a more citrus, herbaceous tonic water that could support similarly structured gins.

The first question you have to ask is this: what kind of herbal notes do you want? Back to our septuagenarian French friend Jacques Touche. He helped us to quickly settle on rosemary, which is well regarded within the flavour industry for having a lot of breadth. Again, it provides the supportive base for the other flavours to work from. For the citrus notes, we chose lemon thyme. With Jacques' assistance, Charles travelled

The vibrant, orange Angostura tree in Argentina.

BARK FOR BITTERS?

The colour of Aromatic Tonic Water might lead some people to think we have simply married our tonic with a famous brand of bitters.

The tonic's pink blush notwithstanding, nothing could be further from the truth. The bitters, which do not contain any angostura bark, are so called because they were originally made in the Venezuelan town of Angostura, which is now known as Ciudad Bolívar.

to the Drôme département in southern France and, among the alpine valleys, Jacques introduced him to a small family business producing and distilling lemon thyme essential oils in boilers fired by bales of dried lavender. The Vidal family are a French family of old. When Charles was there they had four generations of Vidal on the fields of lemon thyme at the same moment. With a gas spectrometer happily sited next to the kitchen range, the accumulated knowledge and skill that they have may not last another 50 years sadly as the lure of the towns pulls the younger generations away. Their superb high-quality lemon thyme oil is then added to the rosemary flavour, and topped off with Algerian geranium to complete the floral notes within our Mediterranean Tonic Water. Mediterranean Tonic represented the first time we had created our "own" type of tonic water and not just put quality back into an existing product.

All in all, the Mediterranean Tonic has turned out to be particularly evocative. Its aromas combine to conjure the sense of a walk on a sun-warmed evening in Italy or southern France. Each step releases a scent of wild herbs that wafts up upon the evening air to remind you that, just a short stroll away, lies dinner. And what would better pique the appetite than a perfect Gin and Tonic?

ULTIMATE CUBA LIBRE

The original rum cocktail, created in Havana at the turn of the 20th century when Coca-Cola was first brought to Cuba. *(Pictured)*

50ml (2fl oz) premium golden rum
200ml (7fl oz) Fever-Tree Madagascan
   Cola
Juice of 2 lime wedges, plus 2 lime
   wedges to garnish

Add all the ingredients to a highball glass filled with ice cubes. Garnish with lime wedges.

ULTIMATE BOURBON & COLA

The subtly sweet vanilla notes of our Madagascan Cola pair perfectly with bourbons, to enhance an iconic American cocktail.

50ml (2fl oz) premium bourbon
200ml (7fl oz) Fever-Tree Madagascan
   Cola
Lime wedge, to garnish

Add all the ingredients to a highball glass filled with ice cubes. Garnish with a lime wedge.

ULTIMATE PINK G&T

Our modern, unique twist on the quintessentially British "Pink Gin" combines aromatic botanicals including cardamom, pimento berry and ginger with fresh citrus and juniper-rich gin. *(Pictured)*

50ml (2fl oz) juniper-rich premium gin (we recommend Plymouth Gin, Sipsmith VJOP or a navy strength such as Bathtub)
Fever-Tree Aromatic Tonic Water, to top up
Generous piece of lemon peel, to garnish

Fill a highball glass with plenty of ice cubes and pour in the gin. Top up with the tonic water, then twist the lemon peel over to release the essential oils and aromas, before dropping it into the glass to garnish.

MEDITERRANEAN VODKA & TONIC

Essential oils from Mediterranean flowers, fruits and herbs transform this simplest of drinks into a complex cocktail with delicate floral notes and a soft bitterness.

50ml (2fl oz) premium vodka
200ml (7fl oz) Fever-Tree Mediterranean Tonic Water
Lemon thyme sprig, or twist of lemon peel, to garnish

Fill a large wine glass or highball glass with plenty of ice cubes. Pour in the vodka and then the tonic water and garnish with a lemon thyme sprig or a twist of lemon peel.

M-G&T-O

The Mojito is an all-time favourite and certainly a classic. Traditionally made with white rum and soda water, we have added a bit of sweet-citric flair with Mediterranean Tonic. The bitterness and depth of flavour complement the tropical intensity of the rum. Mo-G&T-O takes this time-honoured Cuban long drink into a whole new league of flavour. You don't need to be on a beach to enjoy this exotic creation...but all the better if you are! *(Pictured)*

A handful of mint leaves, plus extra
    to garnish
50ml (2fl oz) premium white or golden rum
4 lime wedges
Fever-Tree Mediterranean Tonic Water,
    to top up

Slap the mint leaves to release their aromas, then muddle the rum, lime wedges and mint leaves in the bottom of a highball or collins glass. Fill the glass to the top with ice cubes and top up with the tonic water. Garnish with extra mint.

NEGRONI TWIST

Few drinks have more heritage and class than the classic Negroni. Though its true origins are shrouded in mystery, some say it was born in Florence in the early 20th century. A flapper favourite of the 1920s, this blend fascinated Orson Welles who penned one of the earliest mentions of the cocktail. To add a further twist to this spellbinding mix, we have topped it with Mediterranean Tonic. This reimagination is fun, classy and mischievous – nothing sums up the 1920s more than bending the rules!

25ml (5 tsp) premium gin
25ml (5 tsp) sweet vermouth
15ml (1 tbsp) Campari
10ml (2 tsp) fresh lemon juice
Fever-Tree Mediterranean Tonic Water,
    to top up
Twist of orange peel, to garnish
Lemon thyme sprig, to garnish

Add all the ingredients except the tonic water to a highball glass filled with ice cubes. Top up with the tonic water and garnish with a twist of orange peel and a lemon thyme sprig.

MEDITERRANEAN WHITE PORT & TONIC

A Mediterranean twist on the popular White Port and Tonic. There is an effortlessness about life in Portugal that we wanted to capture in this cocktail and its straightforward name reflects the spirit of the country. When the ingredients are this good, they should speak for themselves and this is a simple combination of white port and Mediterranean Tonic. The warm honey, raisin and toasted almond flavours of the port are enhanced by the lemony flavour of the tonic. It's a beautiful balance and the result is a wonderfully refreshing, crisp cocktail that deserves to be savoured.

125ml (4fl oz) premium white port
125ml (4fl oz) Fever-Tree Mediterranean
    Tonic Water
Lemon wedge, to garnish
Mint sprig, to garnish

Fill a highball glass with ice cubes. Pour in the port and tonic water, then stir vigorously. Garnish with a lemon wedge and a mint sprig, and enjoy!

AA TONIC

This cocktail is a subtle twist on an Americano, utilizing the light bitterness of tonic to lighten the flavour and add sparkle to the drink. I love Negronis, Sbagliati and Americanos so it made sense to add the subtle spice of Aromatic Tonic to the base, along with a dash of clove and cinnamon from the bitters. These earthy notes add complexity and an exotic spicy element.

20ml (4 tsp) Campari
20ml (4 tsp) Martini Rosso Vermouth
100ml (3½fl oz) Fever-Tree Aromatic
   Tonic Water
2 dashes of Angostura Bitters
Twist of orange peel, to garnish

Pour all the ingredients in order into a wine glass over ice cubes. Garnish with a twist of orange peel.

CAFÉ CUBANO

While a dark rum mixed with a coffee-enhanced tequila might seem unusual, this spicy yet smooth blend is guaranteed to excite the taste buds. The world-famous Patrón Tequila hails from the heart of Mexico. Over 2,100km (1,300 miles) east lies the spiritual home of Havana Rum – with its superb extra-aged 7 Year bringing deep complexity to this blend. Befitting of this multicultural medley, we have tied it together with elegantly spicy cola. A complex set of 20 ingredients, including Madagascan vanilla, Indonesian nutmeg and Jamaican allspice, lift and harmonize the exotic mix.

100ml (3½fl oz) Fever-Tree Madagascan Cola
25ml (5 tsp) Havana Club 7 Year Old Rum or other premium dark rum
25ml (5 tsp) Patrón XO Cafe, or other coffee liqueur
Grated nutmeg, to garnish

Pour all the ingredients in order into a highball glass over lots of ice cubes. Sprinkle with grated nutmeg to garnish.

TARHUN COLLINS

This drink is named after the ancient Anatolian god of weather. Tarhun also happens to be a popular name for tarragon in some languages and this is one of the main ingredients in the cocktail. The green, herbal and vegetal notes found in Fever-Tree Mediterranean Tonic and Tarquin's Cornish Gin led me to be inspired to create a refreshing Collins-style drink with a bitter finish – something refreshing and moreish. The bitterness is complemented by the herbal notes of the Suze and tarragon, while the grapes add sweetness.

1 tarragon sprig, plus a sprig to garnish
6 large green grapes
30ml (2 tbsp) Tarquin's Cornish Gin
30ml (2 tbsp) Lillet Blanc
30ml (2 tbsp) Martini Bianco Vermouth
10ml (2 tsp) Suze Bitters, or 5ml (1 tsp) Angostura Bitters
20ml (4 tsp) fresh lime juice
30ml (2 tbsp) Fever-Tree Mediterranean Tonic Water

Muddle the grapes and tarragon together in the bottom of a mixing glass. Shake all the ingredients except the tonic water in a cocktail shaker, then double-strain into a collins glass over ice cubes. Top up with the tonic water and garnish with a sprig of fresh tarragon.

SIRIUS FIZZ

This elegant cocktail gets its name from the naval ship HMS *Sirius*. White rye whiskey forms the foundation of the drink with the fruity addition of the iconic Campari liqueur adding fun and colour to the creation. It also adds sweetness and there's more to come with the apricot jam – a good heaped bar spoon is required. There is just enough egg white to add a rich, creamy texture and this, combined with the fizzy tonic, results in a frothy top that is pleasing to the eye and the palate.

1 heaped tsp apricot or peach jam
40ml (1¼fl oz) white rye whiskey
10ml (2 tsp) Campari
25ml (5 tsp) fresh lemon juice
5ml (1 tsp) egg white
30ml (2 tbsp) Fever-Tree Mediterranean
    Tonic Water

Fill a cocktail shaker with ice cubes. Add the rest of the ingredients, except the tonic water, in order. Shake and strain into a highball glass, then add ice cubes and the tonic water.

White Rye, often nicknamed "white dog", is simply rye whiskey that has not been aged in oak and retains quite a bold, spicy character.

TARRAGON & POMEGRANATE FIZZ

I love the smell of tarragon and how it can introduce subtle anise flavours into drinks through a garnish. So I started with tarragon and tried to create a drink that is balanced by the bitterness of the tonic and the anise of the tarragon. This is a really good drink to prepare for anyone who's not quite sure what they'd like – it's long and fruity with a nice balance of acidity and spice to keep you going back for another sip.

30ml (2 tbsp) vodka

10ml (2 tsp) peach schnapps

10ml (2 tsp) pomegranate juice

10ml (2 tsp) fresh lime juice

100ml (3½fl oz) Fever-Tree Aromatic
    Tonic Water

Tarragon sprig, to garnish

Lime wedge, to garnish

Pour all the ingredients in order into a highball glass over ice cubes. Garnish with a tarragon sprig and a lime wedge.

HEARTSTARTER #24

The name came about via the link to the original coffee pick-me-up, The Stimulator, by Dick Bradsell, and the Corpse Reviver series of drinks – and 24 was the number on my football shirt when I was growing up. An alternative to the regular Espresso Martini, this could work both as a refreshing Spritzer or as a dry digestif. Using Panamanian, mild-roasted coffee beans, the pecan, hazelnut and toffee notes pair beautifully with the lemon thyme and rosemary flavours of the tonic. This is coupled with the smoky, fresh and vibrant notes of Botanist Gin. The Heartstarter #24 is designed to be enjoyed in the sun or after dessert.

30ml (2 tbsp) The Botanist Gin
45ml (3 tbsp) Panamanian cold-dripped
    coffee, or 30ml (2 tbsp) cold espresso,
    or shop-bought cold-pressed coffee
15ml (1 tbsp) Solerno Blood Orange
    Liqueur, or Cointreau
Fever-Tree Mediterranean Tonic Water,
    to top up
Rosemary sprig, to garnish

Pour all the ingredients into a highball glass filled with ice cubes. Garnish with a rosemary sprig.

Bar: HEDONIST DRINKS — LEEDS, UK

Bar person: TOM FINNON

PORT BATANGA

I came across an experimental port-cask-finished tequila made by Herradura a few years ago and it blew my mind. Creating a simple cocktail that captures this pairing was the idea behind the drink. The more pronounced cola note of Fever-Tree Madagascan Cola mixes beautifully with sweet ruby port and the earthy undertones of the tequila. For those who like a little heat, you can rim the glass with salt and chilli flakes. *(Pictured)*

4:1 mix of salt and chilli flakes (optional)
40ml (1¼fl oz) tequila (El Jimador Reposado is great; Tapatio Reposado is perfect)
10ml (2 tsp) González Byass Pedro Ximénez Sherry, or any sweet sherry
Fever-Tree Madagascan Cola, to top up
Orange wedge, to garnish

Wet the rim of a tumbler and dip into the salt and chilli mix. Pour the tequila and sherry into the glass over ice cubes. Top up with the cola and garnish with an orange wedge.

GROWN-UP CHERRY COLA

A perfect balance between rich sloe and cherry sweetness, smooth vanilla and tart citrus, this mixture is inspired by the classic confectionery of childhood. You can adjust the sweetness to suit your personal preference by adding a smaller or larger dash to finish the drink. You could also use regular gin in place of the sloe gin, but the lemon juice does even out some of the sweetness so taste as you build the cocktail to ensure the correct balance.

25ml (5 tsp) premium cherry liqueur
50ml (2fl oz) premium sloe, or regular, gin
25ml (5 tsp) fresh lemon juice
1 dash of Fever-Tree Madagascan Cola
Cocktail cherry, to garnish
Dash of Angostura Bitters, to garnish

Shake all the ingredients except the cola in a cocktail shaker over lots of ice cubes and strain into a chilled cocktail glass. Top up with the cola. Garnish with a cocktail cherry and a dash of bitters.

MEDITERRANEAN SOUR

This isn't a drink for the faint-hearted: with its bold flavours and creative decoration, it's a cocktail to be sipped and savoured. The Italian liqueur, Disaronno Amaretto, adds its distinctive almond taste and forms the base of the drink. Lemon juice adds a hint of sourness and this is counteracted by the addition of sugar syrup. Egg white binds this eclectic mix together and the final flourish is a dash of truffle olive oil, which ensures the provenance is truly Mediterranean.

50ml (2fl oz) Disaronno Amaretto

20ml (4 tsp) fresh lemon juice

10ml (2 tsp) simple sugar syrup (*see* page 13)

20ml (4 tsp) egg white

5ml (1 tsp) truffle olive oil

Fever-Tree Mediterranean Tonic Water, to top up

Edible flower, or rosemary sprig, to garnish

Add all the ingredients except the tonic water to a cocktail shaker with ice and shake well. Strain into a rocks glass over ice cubes. Top up with the tonic water and garnish with an edible flower or rosemary sprig.

AS WE DREAM WELL

For the last two summers we have sold a huge number of Aperol Spritzes at K-Bar and we felt the need to come up with an alternative that would be unique to us. We've used Suze Bitters and these are built up with cherry liqueur and white wine. The drink is topped with tonic for a sparkling and refreshing drink that is served in a large red wine glass and garnished with fragrant fresh basil leaves, kumquat slices and some lemon peel.

30ml (2 tbsp) Suze Bitters, or Aperol

30ml (2 tbsp) Cherry Heering (Peter Heering), or any cherry liqueur

50ml (2fl oz) dry white wine

100ml (3½fl oz) Fever-Tree Mediterranean Tonic Water

To garnish

5 basil leaves

1 kumquat, sliced

3 pieces of lemon peel (from ½ a lemon)

Put several large ice cubes and the garnish ingredients into a large red wine glass. Add the rest of the ingredients in order, topping up with the tonic water at the end and stirring to combine.

SAINT BAVARIAN SAGE

This cocktail is inspired by "after-Oktoberfest-flu" that can only be cured by the healing effect of Saint Bavarian Sage. Many people suffer after partying too hard during this famous celebration and this is a good way to ease yourself back to good health with sugar, lemon and enough gin to perk you up. Fever-Tree Mediterranean Tonic Water adds the fizz, while sage helps with the restorative process.

50ml (2fl oz) Edinburgh dry gin, or other gin
30ml (2 tbsp) fresh lemon juice
20ml (4 tsp) icing sugar
7 sage leaves, plus a sprig to garnish
Fever-Tree Mediterranean Tonic Water, to top up
Lemon slice, to garnish

Put all the ingredients except the tonic water into a cocktail shaker and shake well. Strain into a highball glass filled with ice cubes, top up with the tonic water and garnish with a sage sprig and a lemon slice.

Edinburgh Distillery has two stills. One pot still named Flora and a column still named Caledonia.

PREMIUM GRAND TONIC

Elephant Gin has apple and fruity scents with a dry taste and I have added a little apple juice to emphasize them. The drink is finished with Grand Marnier and cucumber slices to complete the elegant and fresh taste. This is an ideal daytime drink, enjoyed as an apéritif, or after a meal when you want to linger and relax over a drink. You can also prepare it for parties – we use a Champagne coupe glass to add an elegant touch.

30ml (2 tbsp) Elephant Gin

10ml (2 tsp) Grand Marnier

3 slices of cucumber, plus an extra slice to garnish

10ml (2 tsp) fresh apple juice

60ml (4 tbsp) Fever-Tree Mediterranean Tonic Water

Twist of orange peel, to garnish

Put all the ingredients except the tonic water into a cocktail shaker and shake well. Strain into a Champagne coupe or cocktail glass and top up with the tonic water. Garnish with a cucumber slice and twist of orange peel.

MADAGASCAN DUSK

Madagascar has long been home to the world's most highly prized and expensive vanilla. Our cola incorporates the rich sweetness of this vanilla, making it an excellent pairing with white rum. Grapefruit juice brings refreshing acidity and fruit (as well as a subtle pink hue). This sharpness, contrasting with the indulgent rum and spicy cola, balances the cocktail perfectly. Plenty of ice and desiccated coconut to garnish will make anyone drinking this cocktail feel like they are on a sandy beach in the Caribbean.

100ml (3½fl oz) fresh pink grapefruit juice
100ml (3½fl oz) Fever-Tree Madagascan Cola
50ml (2fl oz) premium white rum
Orange slices, to garnish
Desiccated coconut, to garnish

Pour the ingredients in order into a highball glass over ice cubes. Garnish with slices of orange and a sprinkle of desiccated coconut.

VANILLA RAISIN FLOAT

The cola in this cocktail has been specially developed to complement spirits and it works incredibly well here to bring out the characteristics of the bourbon. These include vanilla notes, which is why this adult version of the coke float is such an incredible taste sensation. A cooling, fun drink for a hot day, the raisin element comes from the sherry and you can add some extra sweetness with a cherry syrup drizzle over the finished drink. *(Pictured)*

30ml (2 tbsp) Woodford Reserve Bourbon
10ml (2 tsp) González Byass Pedro
    Ximénez Sherry, or any sweet sherry
Fever-Tree Madagascan Cola, to top up
1 scoop of vanilla ice cream
Fresh cherry, to garnish
Cherry syrup, to garnish

Pour the bourbon and sherry into a highball or sling glass over ice cubes, then top up with the cola. Add the ice cream on the top, then garnish with a cherry and a drizzle of cherry syrup.

CASK HIGHBALL

The name refers to the cask ageing of both the base spirit and the sherry in this drink. I love highball-style cocktails in summer – the nuttiness of sherry is delightful with the bitterness of tonic, so that was the starting point. I then added bourbon, as there is sweetness here that works very well with sherry. It's a simple list of ingredients but the end result is a sophisticated drink.

40ml (1¼fl oz) Maker's Mark Bourbon
20ml (4 tsp) Amontillado sherry
100ml (3½fl oz) Fever-Tree Aromatic
    Tonic Water
Twist of orange peel, to garnish

Pour all the ingredients in order into a highball glass over ice cubes. Garnish with a twist of orange peel.

OKINAWA ICED TEA

Okinawa is an island in Japan and has a very beautiful long beach, which seemed like the perfect inspiration for this gorgeous drink. Okinawa Iced Tea is like a Long Island Iced Tea but we use Japanese yuzu sake instead of tequila. The original is an absolute classic, which pairs well with fresh lime or yuzu. There is a subtle sweetness to the drink but the addition of Fever-Tree Madagascan Cola means the botanicals replace a lot of the sweetness and the cocktail is more complex in flavour.

10ml (2 tsp) white rum
10ml (2 tsp) gin
10ml (2 tsp) vodka
10ml (2 tsp) triple sec, or any curaçao
20ml (4 tsp) yuzu sake, or 10ml (2 tsp) sake and 10ml (2 tsp) yuzu or lemon juice
Fever-Tree Madagascan Cola, to top up
Lime wedge, to garnish

Pour all the ingredients except the cola into a cocktail shaker with ice and shake. Strain into a tall or highball glass over ice cubes. Top up with the cola and some ice and garnish with a fresh lime wedge.

Triple sec is an orange flavoured liqueur most commonly used as a cocktail ingredient. While its exact origins are unknown, it was likely first made in France in the mid 19th century.

INDEX

GLOSSARY

All recipes serve one unless otherwise stated.

The quality of a drink is dependent on the quality of its ingredients and many of our contributors have recommended their preferred brands for the spirits used in their recipes. If a particular brand of spirit is not available, please substitute for another premium quality version of the same spirit.

GLOSSARY

UK	US
Beetroot	Beet
Blitz	Process or blend, as when using a food processor or blender
Calvados	Apple brandy
Cocktail stick	Cocktail pick or toothpick
Cordial	Fruit-based syrup, usually diluted with a liquid, such as water, for drinking or used in desserts undiluted
Coriander, fresh	Cilantro
Crème de cassis	Blackcurrant syrup
Demerera	A type of raw sugar; you can use light brown sugar as a substitute
Desiccated coconut	Dry unsweetened coconut
Icing sugar	Confectioners' sugar, also known as powdered sugar
Infuse	Steep
Jam	Preserves
Leaf of gelatine	Gelatin sheet
Moreish	Irresistable
Muscovado	A type of unrefined raw sugar; you can use dark brown sugar as a substitute
Spirit(s)	Alcohol, depending on use of the word
Tumbler	Glass for everyday drinking that lacks a foot or stem
Vanilla pod	Vanilla bean

ACKNOWLEDGEMENTS

There are a lot of people we need to thank who worked tirelessly to bring this book together. However, first and foremost it would be remiss to not mention all those bartenders around the world who took the time and trouble to contribute their amazing recipes to bring this book to life. Without the support of such an innovative group dedicated to their craft, this book would not have been possible.

At Fever-Tree HQ Saskia Meyer not only initiated the project but managed it with endless enthusiasm and optimism through the ups and downs and, again, the book would not be possible without her work. Thank you as well to Andrew Harris for coordinating the gathering of the recipes and to Vince Lawson, Anita Hawk, Craig Harper and Charlie Shotton, the latter testing every recipe in the book. The wider team also helped support the project as always with great flexibility and fervour, so thank you to them and all of Fever-Tree's partners around the world who helped liaise with the bartenders.

Last but by no means least, we must acknowledge Octopus HQ and all those who were involved from the publisher's side. Thank you to head publisher Denise Bates who has been a central pillar to the project and a never-ending source of expert advice. Her calm persistence, tremendous knowledge and passion guided the project and kept it on-track. Thanks as well to Pauline Bache, Sarah Ford and Yasia Williams for countless hours of work and patience throughout, and to Paul Winch-Furness, Allan Stone, Missy Flynn and Jennifer Kay for their help and creativity on the photoshoot.